SO-BKK-691

Pontiac models from 1970 to 1980

Astre	**1975-1977**
Bonneville	**1970-1980**
Catalina	**1970-1980**
Executive	**1970**
Firebird	**1970-1980**
Grand Prix	**1970-1980**
Grandville	**1971-1975**
LeMans	**1971-1980**
Phoenix	**1977-1979**
Sunbird	**1976-1980**
Tempest	**1970**
Ventura	**1971-1977**
Wagons	**1970-1980**

Pontiac
Car Care Guide

Other titles from

BASIC CAR CARE ILLUSTRATED
BODYWORK & PAINTING
TUNEUP & TROUBLESHOOTING
CAR CARE GUIDES:

Buick
Chevy
Chrysler/Plymouth/Dodge
Datsun
Ford/Mercury Compacts
Ford/Mercury Intermediate/Full Size
GM X-Bodies
Honda
Oldsmobile
Toyota
Vega
VW Beetle
VW Rabbit

STAFF AND CONTRIBUTORS

Allen Bragdon, Editor-in-Chief
Jacquelyn Crete, Project Director
Robert Freudenberger, Technical Writer
Nanci Hollas, Managing Editor
John Clement, Editor
Jay Iorio, Associate Editor
Jorge Fonseca, Art Director
Carol Colton, Studio Manager
Michael Eastman, Art Director
Robert Janes, Art Editor
Jane H. Terpening, Art Editor
David Terrio, Art Editor
John B. Miller, Designer
Jeff Mangiat, Illustrator
David Arky, Photographer

The editors are grateful for the assistance
provided by Mr. Robert Klungian, GM Public
Relations, and by Mr. Jack De Nalfo, Circle
Pontiac, Bayside, NY.

Published by Hearst Books
A Division of The Hearst Corporation
224 W. 57th Street
New York, NY 10019

Also published by The Hearst Corporation

MOTOR Auto Repair Manual
MOTOR Imported Car Repair Manual
MOTOR Truck Repair Manual

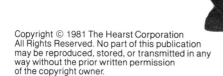

The information herein has been compiled from
authoritative sources. While every effort is made
by the editors to attain accuracy, manufacturing
changes as well as typographical errors and
omissions may occur. The publisher and the
editors cannot be responsible nor do they assume
responsibility for such omissions, errors or
changes.

Manufactured in the United States of America
by The Hearst Corporation
New York, NY 10019

Library of Congress
Catalog Card No. 80-85174

ISBN No. 0-87851-955-9

Car Care Guide

Pontiac

Contents

Foreword

This is a Pontiac book

If you own a Pontiac model—of those models listed on page 1 from 1970 to 1980—this book is for you. It tells you—model by model, year by year—how to keep your car going longer and at lower cost. It won't be of much use to the owners of Chevettes or Fords or Porsches. It was written by a Pontiac expert, illustrated with photos and drawings of Pontiacs. It's a Pontiac book. Period.

When we, the editors, were assigned to this job by Popular Mechanics and MOTOR Manuals, we set out to produce a series of individualized Car Care Guides. We started by drawing up a master list of all repair and maintenance jobs that the do-it-yourselfer (even the first-time do-it-yourselfer) can handle. Then we matched that list with the peculiarities of each make and model. We looked for such factors as accessibility of components, ease of removal and installation, risk of damage or injury. Pontiac owners are fortunate in that the machine they drive is a simple one: no exotic hardware or hard-to-get parts. Just right for the home mechanic!

Then we hired an expert on the Pontiac line who knows the cars inside out. His job was to prepare step-by-step instructions in clear, simple language for each job the Pontiac owner can handle successfully in his or her home garage. After that, he guided our photographers and artists in gathering and preparing the 300-plus illustrations that demonstrate this "hands-on" technique step by step. Finally, when the pages were laid out, our technical experts checked them before they were printed, to make sure everything had been assembled correctly.

How to Use This Book

Chapters Two through Twelve, more than half this book, show how to perform each of the operations in a full engine tuneup. That's where the biggest payoff is in fuel economy and labor costs. *Maintenance* is the key to getting the best performance from your car. To *keep* your Pontiac tuned up you have to make adjustments much more frequently than you must, say, install a new set of disc brakes. The first twelve chapters are arranged in the order you should work to perform an engine-maintenance tuneup. Each chapter covers a different operation. Each operation is described step by step.

The balance of the chapters show how to diagnose problems, and how to disassemble, replace, and reassemble components that can wear out or break in your Pontiac suspension, brakes, and other systems. At the beginning of each chapter we provide a big exploded-view drawing that shows where all the parts are and what they are called. You will find a listing of the tools you *must* have ready to do this job and other tools that are handy because they make the work easier, but are not essential. You won't need a whole garageful of tools and you probably already own many of those you absolutely must have. Generally we have avoided the use of special tools. Jacks, lifting devices, and very heavy, bulky, and limited-use tools can often be obtained at local rental centers.

Check the "Pro Shop" tips scattered throughout the book. These are shortcuts and professional hints that our editors picked up from the pros who do these jobs every day. We've also provided "Econotips" in most chapters. These fuel-saving tune-up and driving recommendations should help you save money on that ever more precious commodity, gas.

To find the page on which instructions for a particular repair job appear in this book, look in the Table of Contents in the front or in the Index in the back.

A note on safety: When you undertake a job, be sure to work slowly and carefully. We've printed *CAUTIONS* about procedures which might be hazardous to you in *italics.*

🛑 signs warn you of any steps which require care to avoid damage to a part of your car.

You can start saving money by improving performance the moment you start putting this book to work on your Pontiac. It was made to be a working partner (even the glue in the spine is formulated to resist cracking when the book is laid open on the car fender). Happy motoring.

The Editors

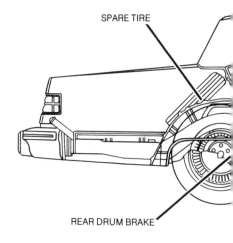

SPARE TIRE

REAR DRUM BRAKE

Know Your Car

Your car is composed of a variety of systems, each with many operating parts. Through normal usage, many of the 15,000 or more parts in your car gradually deteriorate. Some parts wear out sooner than others because they work harder, while many can last the lifetime of the car.

The performance of each system, such as charging, starting, cooling and brakes, depends not only on the condition of all its own parts, but also on the proper functioning of other related systems. If, for example, a hose breaks in the cooling system, the overheating that results can damage the engine.

As systems begin to fail, your driving attitudes may change. Most drivers tend unconsciously to adjust their driving habits. When the brakes show signs of going soft, do you begin to pump them? Or, if the car is pulling to one side, are you correcting for it by steering differently? Keep in mind that you are dealing with a potentially hazardous condition that should be corrected by repairs or adjustments to the car, not by adjusting your driving habits. By familiarizing yourself with the basic systems that make your car run, you will be able to identify and correct many problems before they become costly and possibly dangerous.

To check and protect the systems in your Pon-

tiac, you should follow certain periodic procedures. There are three separate (though related) aspects of car care: tuneup, maintenance, and troubleshooting.

Tuneup is a series of procedures that restore optimum performance, reduce exhaust emissions, and increase your gas mileage. You should tune up your Pontiac at regular intervals rather than waiting for a failure.

Maintenance is a series of procedures (sometimes including tuneup) that ensure that the various systems in your car operate as well, as safely, and as long as possible.

Troubleshooting is a procedure through which your car's ailments are diagnosed and tracked down. The symptoms are analyzed and the possible causes uncovered. Often the cure will require a tuneup, either because the out-of-tune parts were the cause of the problem or because the real cause can only be discovered after the car is properly tuned. Tuneup and routine maintenance can help you avoid having to troubleshoot a problem. Also, if your car is routinely tuned and maintained, when a problem does occur a number of the possible causes will already have been eliminated.

But why are tuneup and maintenance important

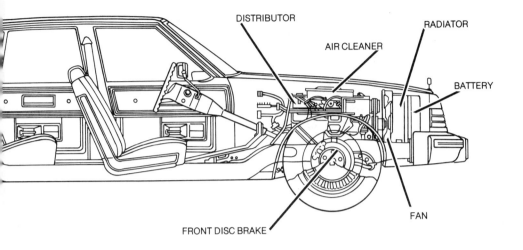

DISTRIBUTOR

AIR CLEANER

RADIATOR

BATTERY

FAN

FRONT DISC BRAKE

for a car that has been running well for a number of months without any evident problems? First, even though a car might sound and run fine, it is going through a continuous process of wear. Modern automobiles operate at high temperatures and friction—the rubbing of metal against metal—is continually created. Eventually all of the moving parts on a car wear out because of friction, heat, and contamination. This is where tuneup and maintenance enter the picture. If a car is poorly maintained, some parts wear out after 30,000 or even 20,000 miles, while with proper maintenance the same parts might last for 100,000 or 150,000 miles.

A poor tuneup or dirty engine oil can cause major damage to the engine. Poorly maintained coolant or a loose fan belt may cause the engine to overheat. As a result, it may be necessary to rebuild or replace the entire engine, at a considerable cost. And the life of many systems on a car, such as brakes, clutch, or suspension and steering, can be dramatically extended by simple and routine checks and adjustments. So a major reason for following regular tuneup and maintenance procedures is to increase the longevity of your car and therefore save money.

Tuneup and maintenance also ensure that your engine will operate at maximum capability and efficiency. An out-of-tune car will consume too

much fuel and perform poorly. And at today's fuel prices, it is certainly worth it to spend the time and the cost of tuneup parts to get optimum gas mileage.

Finally, through routine maintenance you can usually avoid brake failure, tire blowouts, stalling on a bridge or highway, overheating in crowded city traffic, and a host of other unexpected and potentially dangerous situations.

Although how well your car runs and how long it lasts are undeniably important considerations, perhaps the most important is its reliability—how sure you can be that you will reach your destination safely.

If you have never worked on your own car, it may at first appear to be a very mysterious machine. All of those hoses, cans, tubes and belts often cause beginners to throw up their hands and forget the idea of ever doing it themselves. But don't give up! With a little help you can figure out how most of the systems work and which ones you can work on. The first step is to introduce yourself to your Pontiac. Examine what's under the hood, look underneath the front and rear ends, and locate the major systems and parts. The drawings at the beginning of each of the following chapters will guide you in getting to know your car.

BATTERY

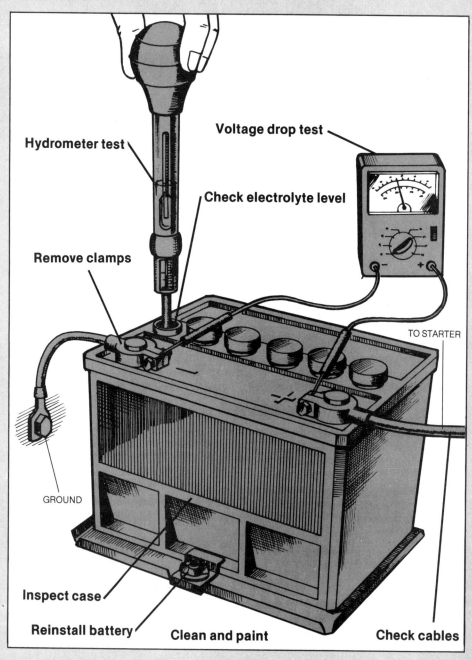

Hydrometer test

Voltage drop test

Check electrolyte level

Remove clamps

TO STARTER

GROUND

Inspect case

Reinstall battery

Clean and paint

Check cables

2

Battery and Cable Service

1 **Inspect case.** Place a fender cover near the battery and inspect the case and top for cracks, leaks, bulges, warpage, and dirt (p. 12).

2 **Perform hydrometer test.** This measures the specific gravity of the battery's electrolyte. (Note: the test cannot be performed on most maintenance-free batteries). A reading above 1.225 means the battery is OK for further testing, as long as the individual cell readings don't vary more than .050 points from each other. If they do, replace the battery. If the specific gravity is below specs, charge the battery and retest. If the battery fails the test again, replace it (p. 13).

3 **Check cables.** Inspect the cables for breaks and wear. Replace, if necessary (p. 14).

4 **Remove clamps.** Remove the cable clamps from the battery posts. Inspect them and the posts for deposits and corrosion (p. 14).

5 **Clean and paint.** Remove the hold-down clamps and lift out the battery with a strap. Clean the case, top, clamps, and posts. Replace parts as needed. Clean the battery shelf (box) and hold-down clamps and paint with an acid-resistant paint (p. 15).

6 **Reinstall battery.** Return the battery to the box and reinstall the hold-down clamps and battery cables (p. 16).

7 **Check electrolyte level.** Remove all cell caps to make sure the plates are covered with electrolyte. If they are not, add distilled or mineral-free water to each cell that needs electrolyte (p. 16). For maintenance-free batteries, check the visual state-of-charge indicator if your car has one.

8 **Perform load or voltage drop test.** If the voltmeter reading is above 9.5 volts, the battery is OK. If it's not, charge the battery and retest (p.16). If the battery still fails the voltage test, you may have to replace it. But before you do, check the starter.

TOOLS

Essential. Basic tools • Goggles • Fender cover • Hydrometer • Wire Brush • Water (distilled or mineral-free) • Baking soda • Petroleum jelly • Towels or clean rags • Voltmeter • Acid-resistant paint or undercoating.

Handy. Cable terminal puller • Terminal spreader • Jumper cables • Battery post cleaning tool • Terminal adapter (for side-terminal batteries) • Battery charger • Lifting strap • Battery pliers • Remote starter switch.

Inspect case

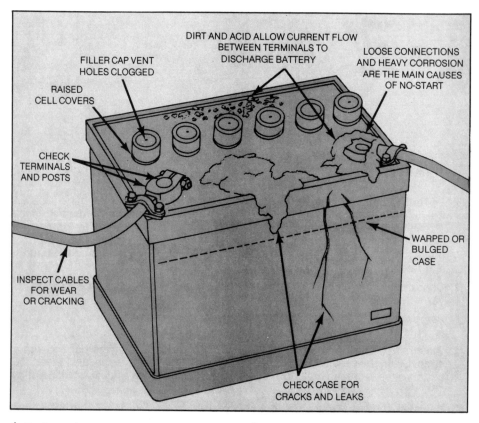

RAISED CELL COVERS

FILLER CAP VENT HOLES CLOGGED

DIRT AND ACID ALLOW CURRENT FLOW BETWEEN TERMINALS TO DISCHARGE BATTERY

LOOSE CONNECTIONS AND HEAVY CORROSION ARE THE MAIN CAUSES OF NO-START

CHECK TERMINALS AND POSTS

INSPECT CABLES FOR WEAR OR CRACKING

WARPED OR BULGED CASE

CHECK CASE FOR CRACKS AND LEAKS

1 Replace a battery which has cracks, leaks, raised cell covers, warpage or bulges.

2 Check for loose connections and heavy deposits and corrosion around the battery posts. This can cause a hard- or no-start condition. Tighten connections and clean to eliminate corrosion, if necessary.

3 Check, and if necessary clean, filler cap vent holes, terminals, and posts.

4 Inspect cables for wear or cracking and replace if necessary.

5 If the top of the battery is dirty or wet or has acid on it, clean it. Current flow between terminals can discharge a battery.

6 If wetness recurs after you have cleaned the top of the battery, there may be other problems, such as a hairline crack in the case or a faulty charging system.

Perform hydrometer test

A battery's acid and water mixture, called electrolyte, is checked with a hydrometer, which measures specific gravity (density or weight). But remember maintenance-free batteries usually do not have removable cell caps, so you cannot perform this test on such batteries.

The tool used for this test consists of a glass tube with a rubber bulb on one end and a hose on the other. The electrolyte is drawn into the tube, and a calibrated float measures specific gravity. A good hydrometer is equipped with a thermometer and a graduated scale to compensate for variations in temperature. It saves the trouble of correcting for temperature.

CAUTION: Electrolyte contains sulfuric acid, so wear protective clothing and goggles when working on a battery. If the electrolyte spills on your hands or face, wash it off immediately and thoroughly with water to prevent acid burn. If it spills on your clothing, wash it out at once or it will burn holes. Any electrolyte spilled on the battery, fender or engine parts must be washed off with water immediately to prevent damage. Rinse the hydrometer out with water when you have finished the test.

1 Remove all caps from the battery cells.

2 Squeeze the hydrometer bulb, then insert the rubber hose into the first cell, keeping the hydrometer straight up.

3 Release the bulb and draw electrolyte into the tube until the float rises freely.

4 Make a note of the specific gravity reading.

5 Empty the electrolyte into the same cell.

6 Test all cells in the same manner and write down the results. A fully charged battery should read 1.280, a half-charged battery should read 1.220, and a dead battery will have a reading below 1.190. These figures depend on the temperature. The standard is 80 °F. Subtract .004 points for every 10 ° below 80 ° and add .004 points for every 10 ° above 80 °. All the cells must be within .050 of each other. If they are not, replace the battery. If the specific gravity is below specs, charge the battery and retest with the hydrometer. If the battery fails the test again, replace it.

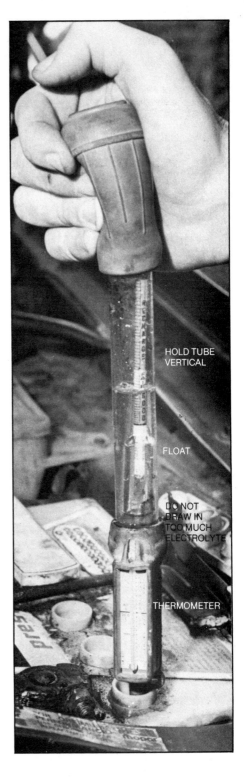

HOLD TUBE VERTICAL

FLOAT

DO NOT DRAW IN TOO MUCH ELECTROLYTE

THERMOMETER

Check cables

Battery cables with high resistance because of wear, cracking, corrosion, or looseness can be a major cause of a no-start condition. This condition may make you think your battery is at fault or even cause you to replace it needlessly. A careful inspection of cables and connections can save you time and maybe money.

1 When the insulation is cracked or frayed, the exposed wire encourages corrosion, which builds up resistance, eats away at the cable, and can cause hard starting. Damaged cables should be replaced.

2 If only the terminal clamp is damaged, you don't have to replace the whole cable. Just cut off the clamp, strip off about 3/4 inch of insulation, clean the cable thoroughly, and install a replacement clamp.

Remove clamps

1 Loosen the cable-clamp retaining bolts with the proper wrench.

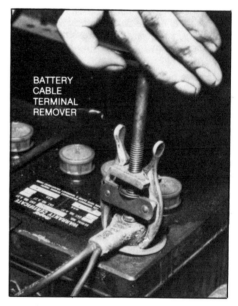

BATTERY
CABLE
TERMINAL
REMOVER

2 Remove the negative cable first. Use a cable terminal puller if the cable terminals are hard to remove. Place the legs of the puller under the cable terminal and tighten the puller screw until the clamp comes off. If you haven't got a puller, open the clamp by twisting the blade of a screwdriver in the seam of the clamp.

🛑 Always remove the negative (−) battery cable first, then the positive (+). When replacing the cables, install the positive first and the negative second. This will reduce the chance of sparks.

How not to blow up your battery

The battery in your car is a potential bomb. If you don't take the proper precautions, it could blow up in your face. The danger is greatest when you are using a charger, boosting a dead battery or boosting a frozen battery.

A battery always has hydrogen gases around the top. Any spark could ignite and explode this gas, so never smoke when working on a battery, and always ventilate the area around it. Remove all the vent caps and cover the openings with a damp cloth. This will act as a flame arrester and allow the gas to pass out.

Charging a battery

Switch on the charger only after all hookups have been made. Connect the positive clamp to the positive post first. Connect the negative clamp to a good ground at least a foot away from the battery. Make sure all electrically operated components are turned off. After charging, switch off the charger before disconnecting the clamps.

Boosting a battery

See the "Jump'er" section in this chapter for guidelines on how to hook up jumper cables.

Clean and paint

1 To remove the battery from the box, disconnect the cables from the battery, making sure all switches and accessories are off.

2 Then remove the hold-down clamps. Before you can budge them, you may first have to remove any rust or corrosion with a wire brush and apply penetrating oil or a baking-soda solution to the bolts.

3 Now remove the battery with a lifting strap —this is the safest way to do it.

4 Mix a solution of baking soda with water. To prevent this solution from getting into the cells, plug each cell cap vent hole with a toothpick.

STOP Even a small amount of baking soda will affect the battery's operation, so be very careful to plug the cell caps well.

5 Brush the mixture on the battery case and in the box. Scrub vigorously, then rinse thoroughly with clean water and wipe dry.

6 Clean the cable terminals and battery posts with a special tool. This tool is used for top-terminal batteries. You can also use it or a small wire brush to clean side-terminal batteries.

7 After cleaning the box and the hold-down clamps, paint them thoroughly with acid-resistant paint or undercoating. This is important because contamination of the box with dirt or acid can promote battery discharge and cause the box to rust away rapidly.

Reinstall battery

1 To reinstall top-terminal cables, you first may have to spread the clamps with a screwdriver or a special spreading tool.

2 Always replace the positive (+) cable first, then the negative cable.

3 After tightening the bolts with the proper wrench and making sure the terminals are tight on the battery posts, coat the terminals with petroleum jelly or heavy grease to retard corrosion. There are also commercially available felt pads treated with oil that you can use in place of the jelly.

Check electrolyte level

1 To check the electrolyte level of your battery, remove all cell caps to make sure all the plates are covered with electrolyte. Do this once a month.

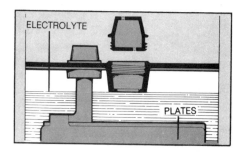

2 If the level is low, fill each cell with distilled or mineral-free water. Make sure the water covers the plates up to a point just below the bottom of the lip at the base of the filler hole, never higher.

OR if your car is equipped with a maintenance-free battery that does not have removable cell caps, and the water level is low, the battery

must be replaced. A sight glass on the top of some maintenance-free batteries lets you check the state-of-charge. Green means OK—the battery can remain in service or is ready for further testing. If the indicator is dark, the battery should be charged until the green dot appears. Light or yellow means the battery must be replaced. In this case, don't perform a load or voltage drop test.

Perform load or voltage drop test

The load or cranking voltage drop test checks the battery's capacity and its ability to deliver and hold the least amount of voltage needed to start your car under all conditions. Before proceeding with this test, make sure the battery has a specific gravity of at least 1.220 at 80°F.

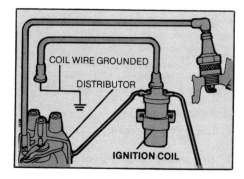

1 Unhook the high voltage coil wire from the center tower of the distributor cap (never from the coil!) so the car won't start while you're cranking the engine. Then ground the coil wire. With electronic ignition (HEI), disconnect the feed wire (pink) from the distributor.

2 Connect the positive lead of the voltmeter to the positive post of the battery and the negative lead to the negative post.

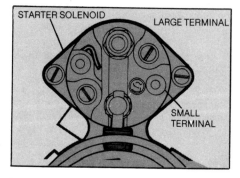

3 If you do not have a helper to sit in the car and crank the engine, connect a remote control starter switch. To hook it up, connect one lead of the switch to the large terminal on the starter solenoid, and the other lead to the small terminal. See the chapter on Starting System Service for more details, or follow the switch manufacturer's instructions.

4 Then crank the engine for about ten seconds. At the same time, observe the voltage reading. It should not drop below 9.5 volts. If it does, the battery may have a weak or defective cell or cells.

5 To check, charge the battery and then retest. If it still reads below 9.5 volts, you may have to replace the battery. But before you do, check the starter (see the chapter on Starting System Service).

Jump'er

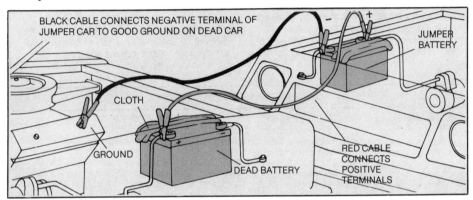

BLACK CABLE CONNECTS NEGATIVE TERMINAL OF JUMPER CAR TO GOOD GROUND ON DEAD CAR

JUMPER BATTERY

CLOTH

GROUND

DEAD BATTERY

RED CABLE CONNECTS POSITIVE TERMINALS

The jumper cable is one of the most frequently used of all automotive accessory tools. Yet many people hook them up incorrectly and damage vital electrical components such as the battery and the alternator, or even injure themselves.

When hooking up battery jumper cables, always trace the negative cable from the battery to its ground. This is the only way to determine for sure which is the negative and which is the positive terminal. A red cable doesn't always mean positive. Be sure before you hook up the jumpers.

1 Connect the red jumper cable to the positive (+) terminal of the battery to be jumped and to the positive terminal of the boosting car's battery.

2 Connect the negative (–) or black jumper cable to the negative terminal of the boosting car.

3 Connect the other end of the negative jumper cable to a good ground (the alternator bracket or a heavy nut or bolt) on the engine of the car to be jumped. Do not connect this end to the negative battery post or you may make a spark that could ignite the hydrogen gas around the top of the battery.

4 Start the engine of the car with the boosting battery and turn on the ignition of the car with the disabled battery.

5 When the disabled car has been started, disconnect the cables, reversing the above order.

Jump-starting an engine with a battery from another car is a common procedure, but one which can be dangerous if precautions are not taken. Follow these rules for hooking up jumper cables:

• Open the hoods of both cars ahead of time to allow the hydrogen to disperse.

• Turn off your ignition and all electrical accessories to avoid draining power that might still be left in the battery.

• Put your transmission in Park (automatic) or Neutral (manual) and your parking brake on.

• Wear eye protection, gloves, and other protective clothing to guard against splashing acid.

• Remove all cell caps from the disabled battery and cover the openings completely with a damp cloth.

• Check the electrolyte level in the cells and add water, if necessary.

• Never jump a battery if the electrolyte is frozen. The battery could explode.

• Don't smoke or hold a flame near the battery.

• Make sure the two cars are not touching.

• Throw away all acid-soaked cloths.

All About Batteries

Charge it!

If your battery ever goes dead, it usually can be recharged. The best way to do this is with a trickle or slow charge of low amperage. With this method there is less wear and tear on the battery and it will take a fuller charge. A slow charger charges about three to six amps and takes more than 16 hours to fully charge a battery. Before charging, prepare the battery by removing the vent caps and adding water, if needed. Connect the positive (+) clamp of the charger to the positive battery terminal and the negative (−) clamp to the negative terminal. Charge until the electrolyte's specific gravity does not increase on three consecutive one-hour readings. Then, cut the charge rate down to its minimum and charge one hour longer. Don't let the battery's temperature exceed 125°F, and don't forget to compensate for temperature.

CAUTION: Charging will release hydrogen gas, which is explosive, so don't smoke or do anything that might make a spark around the

FAST-CHARGE TIMETABLE

FAST-CHARGE TIME	STANDARD SPECIFIC GRAVITY AS USED IN TEMPERATE CLIMATES	SPECIFIC GRAVITY IN CELLS BUILT WITH EXTRA WATER CAPACITY
1 hour	1.150 or less	1.135 or less
¾ hour	1.150 to 1.175	1.135 to 1.160
½ hour	1.175 to 1.200	1.160 to 1.185
¼ hour	1.200 to 1.225	1.185 to 1.210
*slow charge	above 1.225	above 1.210

*In order to fully charge a battery, the period of fast-charge recommended above should be followed by a period of slow-charge until the specific gravity reading indicates a fully charged battery

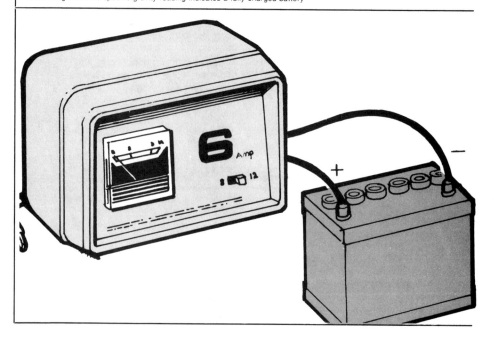

battery. *If battery temperature exceeds 125°F, reduce the charging rate. Unplug the charger before removing the clamps to avoid sparks.*

Prepare a battery for fast-charging the same way you would for slow-charging. To set the charging rate and time period, follow the equipment manufacturer's instructions. If you don't know the rate and time, charge a 12-volt battery at a 35-amp rate for 20 minutes, but don't let the electrolyte temperature go above 125°F. Control the rate so it does not cause excessive gassing and loss of electrolyte. Don't fast-charge a battery for more than one hour without checking the specific gravity. If it shows no significant change after one hour, revert to the slow-charge method. This fast-charge time table should help you out.

About leaky batteries

If one or two battery cells need water more frequently than the others, or if the battery or its box seems to be wet constantly, you may have a cracked or leaky battery case.

To find out for sure, fill the cells to the proper level, then remove the battery from its box and wash it down thoroughly with a solution of baking soda and water (plug the cell cap vents with toothpicks). The battery must be perfectly clean and dry.

Examine the entire case for leaks. Even if you can't see any, there may still be a hairline crack that's too small to be visible, so test further with a voltmeter. Attach the negative lead of the voltmeter to the negative battery post and the positive lead to the blade of a screwdriver. With the meter on the low scale, pass the blade along every area of the case (don't touch the negative post). If the needle jumps, you've found a leak.

Cracks can sometimes be temporarily patched with an acid-resistant sealer, such as roofing tar. The right repair, however, is replacement.

Buying a battery

Let's say you're pretty sure you need a new battery. How do you decide which is the right one for your car? The big question you should ask yourself is: Will the battery deliver on the coldest morning? The amount of power a battery puts out on a zero-degree day is called cold-performance and it is that rating you should be looking at first when shopping for a battery. When the mercury dips to zero, a 60-month battery can shoot around 500 amps to your starter. An 18-month unit, on the other hand, may only be able to provide 240 amps.

How can you tell what your car's cold-cranking requirement is? Simple. Just take the engine's cubic-inch displacement figure and match it with the battery's cold-cranking rating. In cold climates, add 20 percent. For example: You live in Minnesota and drive a model with a 350 cubic inch V-8 engine. You'll need a battery with a basic cold-cranking rating of 350 amps. Therefore, in this case, buy a battery with a cold-cranking rating of not less than 420 amps.

Another rating that tells you about the bat-tery's performance is reserve capacity. That number tells you how many minutes your car can keep running at night if your alternator dies on you. If a battery has a reserve capacity of 100, it means you can drive for 100 minutes on a balmy night without an alternator before the battery stops working altogether.

Once you've checked out cold-cranking and reserve capacity, your next considerations in buying a battery should be warranty and price. If you think you will keep your car longer than the cold-cranking rating dictates, then by all means go to a generous warranty. The longer the warranty, the higher the price.

Battery warranties come in various forms. The most common offer an initial free replacement period of 90 days. After that, the rest of the warranty is broken down and prorated by months. If you buy a 36-month battery for $36.00, each month is worth $1.00. So if your battery fails in 24 months, you have $12.00 worth of credit toward another battery at the same store.

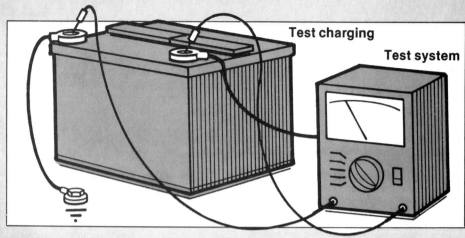

Test charging

Test system

CHARGING

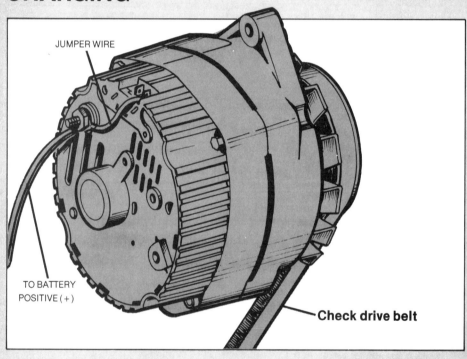

JUMPER WIRE

TO BATTERY
POSITIVE (+)

Check drive belt

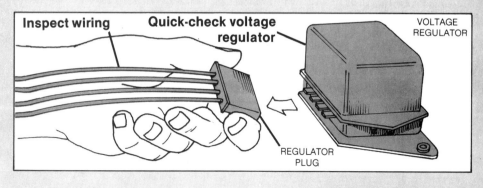

Inspect wiring

Quick-check voltage regulator

VOLTAGE REGULATOR

REGULATOR PLUG

3

Charging System Service

PREP: Check the battery. Make sure it's in a good state of charge.

1 **Test for charging.** First connect a voltmeter to the battery with all accessories turned off and note the voltage. Then start the engine and bring it up to normal operating temperature at fast idle. The voltmeter should now indicate a reading of 13 to 15 volts. If it indicates battery voltage only, the system is not charging (p. 22).

2 **Check drive belt.** Try to turn the alternator pulley by hand. If it moves, the belt is slipping and should be adjusted (p. 24). Repeat the test in step 1.

3 **Inspect wiring.** Check the alternator and regulator wiring for looseness and corrosion. Make sure all the connections are clean and tight and that the alternator and regulator are well-grounded (p. 27).

4 **Quick-check voltage regulator.** Run the engine at a fast idle, 1500 to 2000 rpm, and note the voltmeter reading. If it's higher than the battery voltage reading (see the reading in step 1), let the engine run until the voltage reading reaches its highest value. If the voltage keeps climbing above 15 volts, the regulator is faulty and you should replace it (p. 27).

5 **Test system.** If you encounter a no-charge condition, first check the regulator by bypassing it, then connect a voltmeter to the battery. The meter reading will determine whether the regulator or the alternator is faulty (p. 28).

Essential. Basic tools • Jumper wire • Straightedge • Ruler • Voltmeter.
Handy. Fender cover • Belt tension gauge.

PRO SHOP Unlike a generator, an alternator has no residual magnetism. It can only create a field electromagnetically from current fed to it from the battery. This makes possible a simple check to see if the alternator field circuit is complete. Start the engine and touch the blade of a screwdriver to the back of the housing where the rotor bearing is located. You should feel a strong magnetic attraction. If you don't, then either the field wiring, the regulator, or the rotor and brush assembly is faulty.

Test for charging

The charging system can give years of service with a minimal amount of maintenance. If system failure is suspected, prompt attention and repair may prevent damage to vital electrical components such as the alternator, regulator, battery, and even light bulbs and electrical wiring. If your alternator light or ammeter shows a low-charge, no-charge, or discharge condition, perform this quick test to see if the problem is in the alternator or regulator.

1 Switch your voltmeter to the proper range, then touch the positive (+) lead to the positive battery post and the negative lead (−) to the negative battery post. The meter should read about 12 volts.

2 Start the engine and read the voltage with the meter attached as above. The reading should rise to 13–15 volts. If it doesn't, there is a problem in the alternator or regulator, so go on to the next step.

3 If your car has a Delcotron system with an external regulator, remove the F-R plug located at the top of the alternator, and attach a small jumper wire to the F and BAT terminals. This is known as "full fielding." It bypasses the regulator.

🛑 Do not allow the end of the jumper wire to touch the alternator case or other grounds.

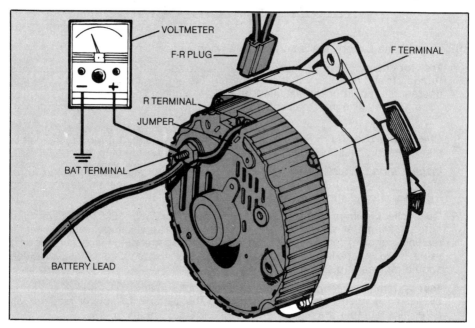

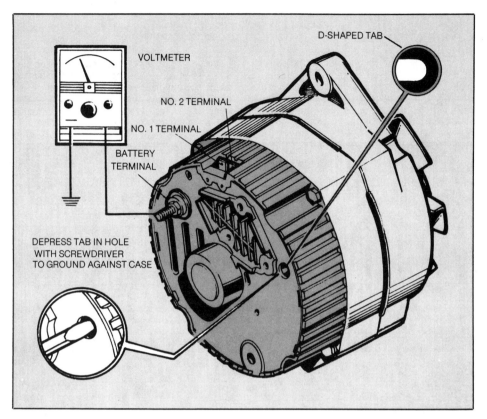

VOLTMETER

D-SHAPED TAB

NO. 2 TERMINAL

NO. 1 TERMINAL

BATTERY
TERMINAL

DEPRESS TAB IN HOLE
WITH SCREWDRIVER
TO GROUND AGAINST CASE

4 If your car has a Delcotron integral regulator system, it is not necessary to disconnect anything to bypass the regulator. Instead, ground the little tab that is inside the hole in the back of the case by inserting the blade of a screwdriver and touching it to both the tab and the case.

5 Attach the voltmeter's positive lead to the alternator BAT terminal and the negative lead to ground.

6 Start the engine. With the F-to-BAT jumper wire in place on external regulator systems, and the tab grounded through the hole on integral regulator systems, the voltmeter should read 15 volts or higher. If it indicates battery voltage only, the alternator is at fault. If the voltage reading is OK, and a no-charge condition was present, the regulator or field circuit is causing the problem.

STOP Do not operate the engine under these conditions any longer than necessary to obtain a voltmeter reading. The alternator, if charging, is running unregulated, and this may overload the car's electrical system and cause damage to its components.

PRO SHOP You can make you own F-R adapter. At an auto salvage yard or auto parts store, purchase an F-R plug. Completely cut off the R wire, then strip about one inch of insulation from the F wire so it can be attached to the BAT terminal. You now have an adapter with which to test your alternator. There will now be less chance of causing a short circuit than if you used a jumper wire.

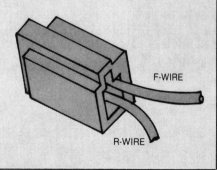

F-WIRE

R-WIRE

Check drive belt

The drive belt must be adjusted to the correct tightness. If it's too loose, it may slip, and your battery might not recharge and so fail to start the engine. If the belt is too tight, it can damage the alternator or water pump bearings. Belts will usually tell you they're too loose by squealing loudly. A loose drive belt usually makes this noise when a cold engine is started, when the car is suddenly accelerated, or when the electrical accessories with a heavy load—headlights, for example—are switched on, because of the magnetic drag in the alternator.

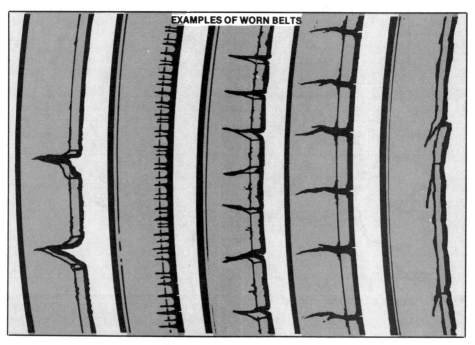

EXAMPLES OF WORN BELTS

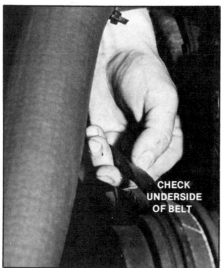

CHECK UNDERSIDE OF BELT

1 Check the drive belt for cracks. Such cracks can be enlarged for inspection by flexing the belt.

2 Check for grease spots. Grease rots ordinary rubber and can damage the belt. Grease on the underside of the belt can cause it to slip during rotation. This has nearly the same effect as a loose drive belt.

3 Check for glazing. A glazed belt with hard surfaces can slip, causing overheating.

4 Always check the underside of the drive belt. Split belts may appear sound from the top but the sides and bottom may be severely split and ready to fail.

5 To check the drive belt for looseness, try to turn the alternator pulley by hand. If it turns, the belt is slipping.

6 To check drive belt tension, bridge the alternator and fan pulleys with a straightedge, and press down on the belt halfway between

the two pulleys with the edge of a ruler. If the belt sags more than half an inch, it's too loose. If you have a belt tension gauge, place it half-way between the alternator and fan pulleys. Instructions for the use of the gauge can usually be found on it.

ABOUT ALTERNATORS An alternator is actually an A.C. generator that uses internal diodes (rectifiers) to convert alternating current to the D.C. voltage a car needs. In an alternator, a magnetic field is produced by windings wrapped around a rotor that spins inside stator windings. Excitor current (which makes the magnetic field) is turned on and off by the voltage regulator in order to control the strength of the magnetic field and hence the amount of power the alternator puts out. The A.C. produced in the stator windings is changed (rectified) to D.C. by three negative and three positive diodes, each of which acts as an electrical one-way valve; by allowing current to pass in only one direction, they convert A.C. to D.C.

To adjust drive belt tension

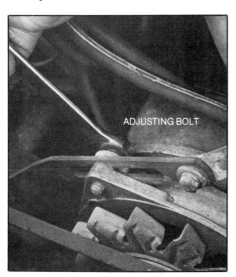

ADJUSTING BOLT

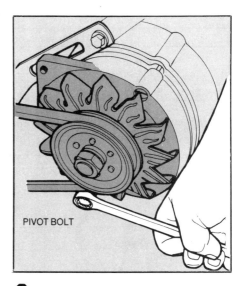

PIVOT BOLT

1 Locate and loosen the adjusting lock bolt on the alternator. The adjusting bolt is in a slotted bracket.

2 Loosen the pivot bolt. This bolt is at the bottom of the alternator on the front and has a nut on the back.

3 To tighten an alternator belt, hold the alternator in a taut position with a pry bar and carefully pry against the alternator case and the engine block.

STOP When you want to move a part with a pry bar, be careful where you position the bar. Do not lean the bar against the alternator fins, and make sure the bar is well-positioned so it does not slip and scrape your knuckles.

4 Check the belt's tension and, when it's correct, tighten the alternator's adjusting bolt and the pivot bolt. Then recheck.

To replace other drive belts

Other belts in the engine compartment—air conditioning, power steering, and air-injection belts—are checked and adjusted in the same manner as previously described. These belts should all be checked periodically and replaced when necessary.

Note: Drive belts are usually adjusted by moving the part that is driven by that particular belt. However, the water pump and fan belts are adjusted by moving the alternator.

1 Disconnect the negative (−) cable at the battery.

2 With the correct size wrenches (1/2- and 9/16-inch), loosen the adjusting and mounting bolts or nuts. Do not remove them.

3 Push the alternator toward the water pump by hand just enough to loosen the belt.

4 Remove the belt from all the pulleys.

🛑 On some models, depending on equipment such as air conditioning, power steering, or air injection pump, it may be necessary to remove other belts first. If so, loosen the unit in the same manner you did the alternator.

5 Install the new drive belt. Be sure the belt is set into each pulley correctly.

6 Carefully place a pry bar or wooden stake between the alternator housing and a suitable metal engine part.

7 Apply moderate pulling or lifting force to the stake. This will move the alternator back to its original position.

8 Tighten the upper adjusting bolt.

9 Check the tension with a straightedge and ruler or a belt tension gauge.

10 Readjust the belt tension if necessary.

11 Reinstall any other belts which were removed, then check and adjust tension.

12 Reconnect the battery negative (−) cable to the battery.

BELT TENSION CHART		
3.8L (229 CID)—V6, 4.4L—5.0L—5.7L—V8—6 in line		
Alternator A.I.R. Pump P/S Pump	50 lb. Min.	Adjust to 75 ± 5 lbs. used Adjust to 125 ± 5 lbs. new
A/C Compressor	65 lb. Min.	Adjust to 90 ± 5 lbs. used Adjust to 140 ± 5 lbs. new
3.8L (231 CID)—V6		
Alternator	65 lb. Min.	Adjust to 80 lbs. used Adjust to 145 lbs. new
P/S Pump A/C Compressor	90 lb. Min.	Adjust to 100 lbs. used Adjust to 165 lbs. new
4.9L—V8 Turbo		
Alternator		Adjust to 75-80 lbs. used Adjust to 110-140 lbs. new
P/S Pump A/C Compressor		Adjust to 100-105 lbs. used Adjust to 135-165 lbs. new

Inspect wiring

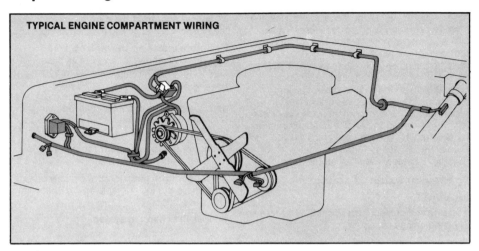

TYPICAL ENGINE COMPARTMENT WIRING

1 Check all connections at the alternator, the voltage regulator, and the wiring harness for looseness and corrosion.

2 Make sure the alternator and the regulator are grounded properly.

3 Check wires for cracks, breaks, or fraying. Frayed wires may accidentally ground, causing the charging system to short out or work overtime.

4 Make sure the alternator mounting bolts are tight and properly grounded.

Check voltage regulator

The procedure for checking the voltage regulator varies depending upon the year of your car. From 1970 through most 1972 models, General Motors installed the Delco-Remy Delcotron alternator with an external voltage regulator. From 1973 to 1980, GM has used the Delcotron

SI alternator with integral regulator. Testing procedures for both systems were explained at the beginning of this chapter. You can replace a faulty external voltage regulator yourself, but the integral type should be left to an expert.

Test system

If you have a no-charge condition, check the system, beginning with the regulator. Bypass it with a jumper wire connected to the F and BAT terminals of the alternator, then connect a voltmeter to the battery. On alternators with integral regulator, bypass the regulator by grounding the tab in the hole in the back of the alternator to the case with the blade of a screwdriver. If the meter now reads two or more volts above battery voltage when the engine is started, the alternator is OK, but the regulator is faulty and should be replaced. If the voltmeter reading does not increase, the alternator is at fault.

To replace external voltage regulator

1 Using the correct size socket, remove the three attaching bolts.

2 Now disconnect the plug by lifting up on the plastic tab and pulling the plug straight out.

3 Before installing the replacement regulator, clean the area where its base comes into contact with the wheel well or radiator support. Use a file or wire brush to remove any rust, paint or dirt. There must be a good metal-to-metal contact between the regulator and the fender well or radiator support.

4 Install the replacement regulator and tighten the attaching bolts securely.

5 Connect the plug. It connects only one way. There is a locator table on the underside of the regulator.

6 Test the charging system.

ABOUT VOLTAGE REGULATORS The field circuit supplies current to the alternator rotor, and this produces the magnetic field that results in the production of power at the alternator output terminal. But if full battery voltage were allowed to excite the field whenever the engine was running, too much current would be produced. This would result in a severely overcharged and ruined battery—the cells would boil themselves dry.

Enter the voltage regulator. This turns the field current on and off so that the alterna-

tor's output is kept within bounds. The mechanical type uses an electromechanically-operated relay to make and break the field circuit. The contacts in the relay are pulled open when a pre-determined amount of current is flowing through the relay's electromagnetic windings. After the contacts open, current drops in the electromagnet until it allows them to close, and the cycle starts again.

Electronic voltage regulators, such as the small integral type found inside later Delco alternators, use switching transistors instead of a relay to control the field current.

PRO SHOP Clean all wire ends before reconnecting them. Also, clean any surface that they come into contact with. This will ensure good electrical connections and reduce electrical resistance. Small knives, small flat files, sandpaper, emery cloth, and wire brushes make excellent cleaning tools.

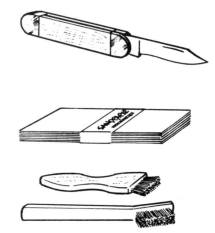

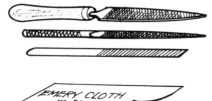

To replace either type of alternator

1 Disconnect the negative battery cable at the battery.

2 Disconnect the F-R or number 1 and number 2 plug from the upper rear of the alternator.

3 Pull back the rubber protective cap if your car is so equipped and remove the nut and wire from the BAT terminal of the alternator.

4 Loosen and remove the alternator belt.

5 Remove all mounting and adjusting bolts holding the alternator to the engine bracket.

🛑 Remove only those mounting and adjusting bolts and nuts necessary to remove the alternator from the engine. The number, location, and size will vary from engine to engine. A simple "look see" will indicate whether or not you need to remove a bolt or nut.

6 Install the replacement alternator and hand-tighten all mounting and adjusting bolts and nuts.

7 Replace and adjust the drive belt.

8 Attach the BAT wire to its terminal on the alternator and securely tighten the nut.

🛑 The wires must be reattached in the correct order to avoid a short circuit and/or damage to the alternator.

9 Replace the protective cap.

10 Next, plug the F-R or number 1 and number 2 plug into its correct position with respect to the locating notch.

11 Reconnect the negative battery cable to the negative battery terminal.

12 Check all bolts, nuts, and connections.

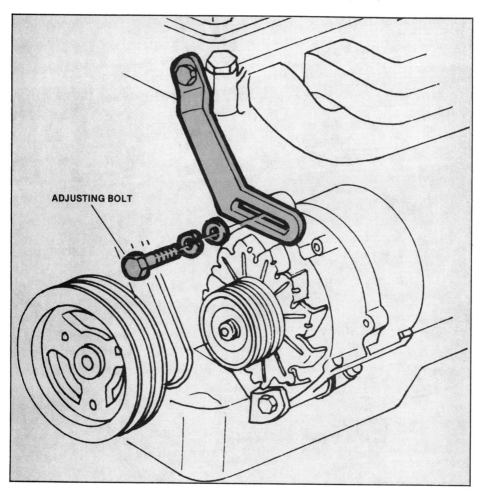

ADJUSTING BOLT

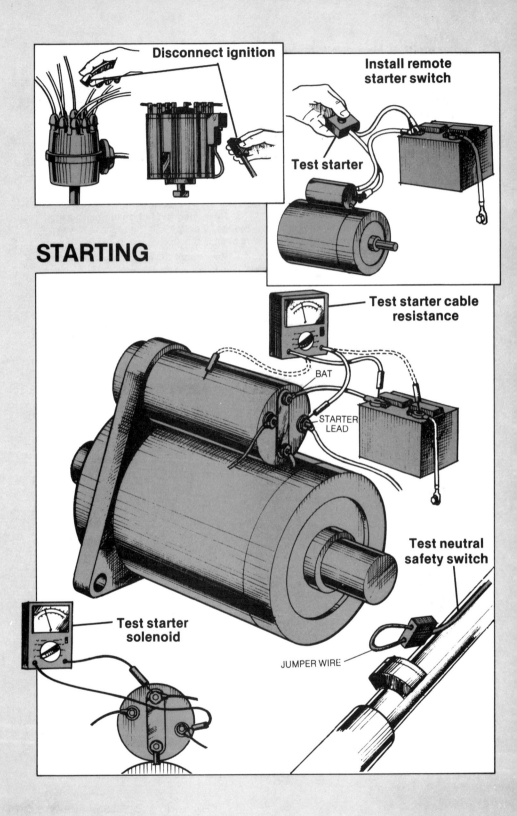

Disconnect ignition

Install remote starter switch

Test starter

STARTING

Test starter cable resistance

BAT

STARTER LEAD

Test neutral safety switch

JUMPER WIRE

Test starter solenoid

4

Starting System Service

PREP: Make sure the battery is in a good state of charge and the cables are tight and free of corrosion. Put the transmission in Neutral (manual) or Park (automatic), then set the parking brake.

1 **Disconnect ignition.** To prevent the engine from starting, remove the coil wire from the center of the distributor cap and ground it with a jumper wire (p. 32). On cars with electronic ignition (HEI), disconnect the feed wire (pink) from the distributor.

2 **Install remote starter switch.** If you don't have a helper to crank the engine from inside the car, you'll need a remote starter switch (p. 33).

3 **Test neutral safety switch.** If the engine doesn't crank in either Neutral or Park, it may be due to a faulty neutral safety switch. To test it, you'll have to bypass it. If the engine starts in any forward gear or in Reverse, the neutral safety switch should be replaced immediately (p. 34).

4 **Test starter cable resistance.** There are three tests you can perform. You'll need a voltmeter calibrated in tenths of a volt (p. 35).

5 **Test starter solenoid.** In a no-crank situation, if the solenoid does not click when the key is turned to the START position, the solenoid may be faulty (p. 36).

6 **Test starter.** You can do this without removing the starter from the car by using the starter solenoid (p. 37).

Essential. Basic tools • Jumper wire • Voltmeter • Safety stands • Jack • Test light.

Handy. Droplight or flashlight • Fender cover • Wire brush or sandpaper • Starter switch.

Disconnect ignition

This is a safety measure to make sure the engine doesn't start during the test.

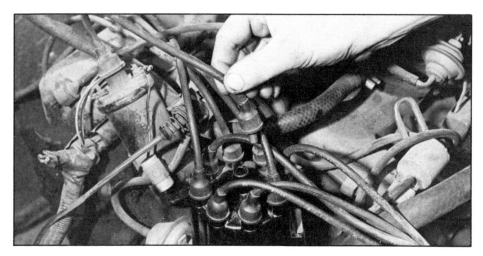

1 Remove the coil wire from the center of the distributor cap and ground it with a jumper wire. The coil wire is the one that goes between the coil and the distributor cap.

🛑 Never remove the wire from the coil's high-tension tower because the spark arcing to the coil primary side could ruin the coil.

2 Connect the jumper wire between the distributor side of the coil wire and any metal part of the engine.

OR if your car is equipped with electronic ignition (HEI), disconnect the feed wire (pink) from the distributor.

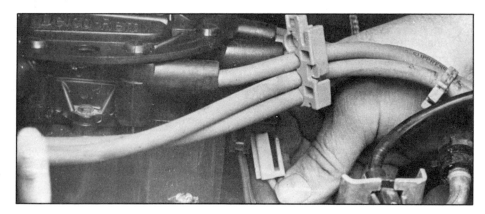

Install remote starter switch

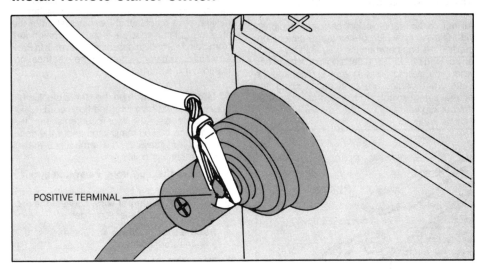

POSITIVE TERMINAL

Since you'll want to observe the starting system components as you test them, you'll need a remote starter switch to enable you to crank the engine from under the hood, if you don't have a helper to sit in the car and crank it.

1 To hook up a remote starter switch, connect one lead of the switch *either* to the large terminal stud on the solenoid that is connected to the heavy cable from the battery *or* to the battery positive terminal.

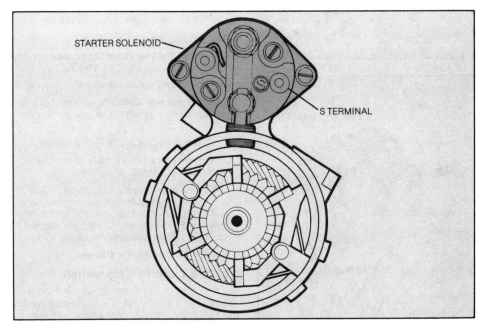

STARTER SOLENOID

S TERMINAL

2 Connect the other lead to the S terminal on the solenoid.

Note: The solenoid is mounted on the starter motor. The S terminal is usually connected to a purple wire.

Test neutral safety switch

All automatic transmission cars are equipped with this switch which prevents the driver from starting the engine when the gear shift lever is in any driving range. If you get a no-crank condition when you attempt to start your engine, and the battery and cables are serviceable, check the neutral safety switch. This switch also operates the backup lights.

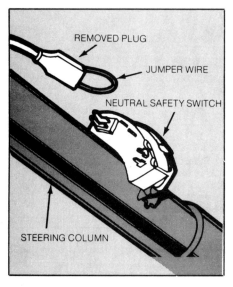

REMOVED PLUG

JUMPER WIRE

NEUTRAL SAFETY SWITCH

STEERING COLUMN

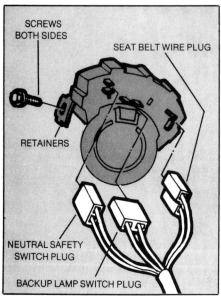

SCREWS
BOTH SIDES

SEAT BELT WIRE PLUG

RETAINERS

NEUTRAL SAFETY
SWITCH PLUG

BACKUP LAMP SWITCH PLUG

Note: On some 1977 and newer models, the safety function of the neutral start switch is fulfilled by a mechanical lockout system in the steering column that prevents the ignition key from being turned unless the shift lever is in Park or Neutral. It has no effect on the electrical activation of the starter.

1 Locate the switch on the steering column under the dashboard near the floorboard.
Note: On models with floor-mounted shifter, the switch is located on the linkage under the console. Testing is basically the same as for the column-mounted switch.

2 Remove the plug from the switch by pulling it back.

3 With a small jumper wire, connect the two left side terminals of the plug together.

4 Set the parking brake and place the shift lever in the Park position.

5 Now start the engine with the ignition switch in the normal manner. If the engine starts, then the neutral safety switch may be defective or out of adjustment.
CAUTION: Remove the jumper wire from the plug as soon as you have completed your testing. With the jumper wire installed in the plug, the engine can start in any gear, causing the car to lunge forward or backward.

To replace safety switch

1 Remove the two attaching screws which hold the safety switch to the steering column.

2 Pull straight up on the switch.

3 Install the new switch, attach the holding screws, and reconnect the plug. It fits into the switch only one way.

4 Start the engine in the Park position.

5 Now switch off the engine and restart it in the Neutral position.

6 Make any necessary adjustment to the safety switch by loosening the two screws and moving the entire switch fractionally either left or right until you are able to start the engine in both the Park and Neutral positions.

7 Securely tighten the screws.

To test clutch safety switch

Some manual transmission models have a safety switch too, but it's connected to the clutch rather than to the transmission linkage. You can test it by similarly bypassing it with a jumper wire.
CAUTION: Make certain the transmission is in Neutral and the parking brake is securely set.

Test starter cable resistance

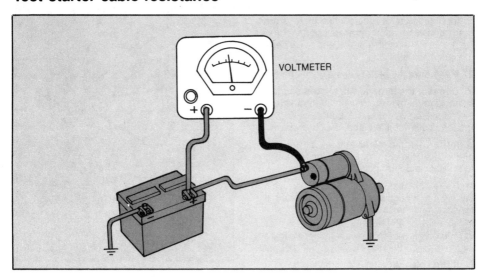

1 Hook up the positive lead of a voltmeter to the battery's positive post and the negative lead of the voltmeter to the BAT terminal on the starter solenoid. Switch to the meter's lowest scale. Crank the engine. The meter should read no more than 0.2 volt. If it is higher, clean and tighten the connections and replace the cable if necessary.

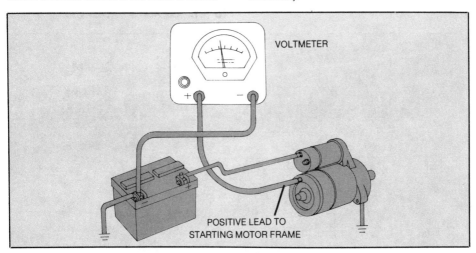

POSITIVE LEAD TO
STARTING MOTOR FRAME

2 To check for high resistance on the grounded side of the starter circuit, connect the negative lead of the voltmeter to the battery's negative post and hold the voltmeter's positive lead to the starter motor housing. Crank the engine. A reading of more than 0.2 volt means there is a lot of resistance in the ground circuit and you should repair it.

3 Connect the negative lead of the voltmeter to the large terminal stud on the starter solenoid that is connected to the heavy cable from the battery. Connect the positive lead of the voltmeter to the motor terminal of the solenoid. Crank the engine and note the voltmeter range. It should not be more than 0.2 volt. If it is, the starter solenoid has high resistance. See the instructions for testing the solenoid.

Test starter solenoid

To test the starter solenoid when there is a no-crank condition, set the transmission in Park or Neutral, set the parking brake, and make certain the ignition is off.

1 **Make sure** the battery has a good charge.

2 **Connect the large terminal stud** on the solenoid to the S terminal with a remote starter switch and press the switch button, or bridge the terminals with the blade of a screwdriver.

3 **If the solenoid clicks** and the starter cranks now, the circuit from the ignition switch to the solenoid S terminal is faulty.

4 **If the solenoid doesn't click,** connect a battery jumper cable between the positive battery post and the solenoid BAT terminal, then bridge the BAT and S terminals again.

🛑 Be careful not to allow the jumper cable clamp to touch the block or any other grounds.

5 **If the solenoid clicks** and the starter cranks now, the circuit between the battery and the large solenoid terminal is at fault.

6 **If there is still no click,** measure the voltage between the solenoid S terminal and ground while the key is held in the START position.

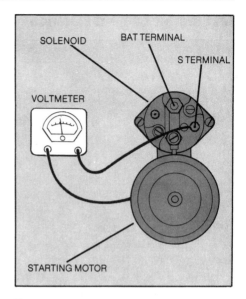

7 **If the voltage is less than 7.7,** the soleno.. control circuit has high resistance.

8 **If the voltage is more than 7.7,** the solenoid should be removed and inspected.

To replace starter solenoid

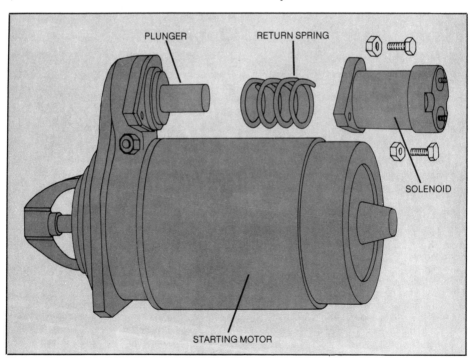

1 Disconnect the negative battery cable
from its post. Identify the solenoid wires so you
can reconnect them correctly.

2 Remove the outer screw and washer from
the motor connector strap terminal, then the
two screws that hold the solenoid housing to

the starter end frame. Twist the solenoid
clockwise to remove the flange key from the
slot in the housing, then lift off the solenoid.

3 Now install the new solenoid and reconnect all the wires. Reconnect the negative battery cable to the post and test for cranking.

Test starter

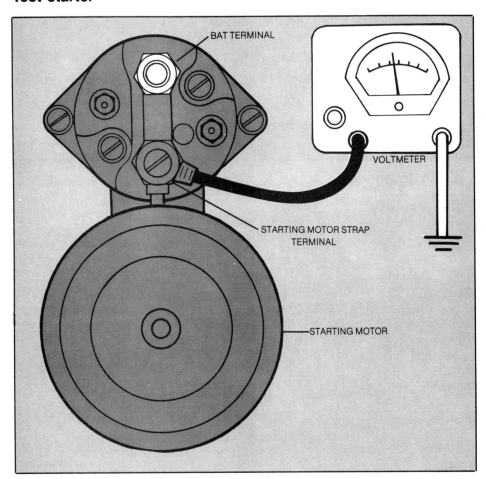

BAT TERMINAL

VOLTMETER

STARTING MOTOR STRAP
TERMINAL

STARTING MOTOR

If the starter cranks slowly, or if the solenoid
clicks and the starter doesn't crank at all, test
the starter motor as follows:

1 Make sure the battery is fully charged.

**2 Connect the positive lead of your
voltmeter** to the motor strap terminal on the
solenoid and the negative lead to ground.

3 Turn the key to START while watching the
voltmeter.

4 If the reading is nine volts or more, and
the starter doesn't crank or cranks slowly, then
the starter has an internal problem and should
be removed to be bench-tested by a professional mechanic.

5 If the reading is less than nine volts, the
problem is in the circuit between the battery
and the solenoid or in the solenoid itself.

To replace starter

1 Disconnect the battery ground cable.

2 Raise the car and support it safely on stands.

3 Disconnect the wires that go to the solenoid and tag them so you can reconnect them properly. Put the nuts and washers back on the terminals.

4 Loosen the starter front bracket bolt or nut, then remove the two starter mount bolts. Remove the flywheel inspection cover if necessary.

5 Remove the front bracket bolt or nut and lower the starter from the engine, front end first (roll it end over end).

6 Put the new starter in place, tighten the vertical mount bolts, then the brace nut or bolt.

7 Reconnect the solenoid terminal leads and battery ground cable.

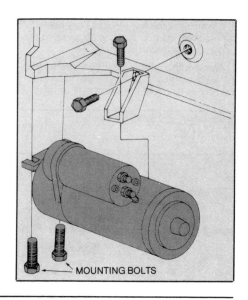

MOUNTING BOLTS

Seatbelt interlock systems

If your car was built in 1974–75, it has a seatbelt interlock system that controls current flow to the solenoid which in turn activates the starter. This means that if your car won't crank and the solenoid won't click, you're going to have to check out the interlock in your search for the problem.

If the trouble is not in the battery, cables, starter motor, solenoid, or neutral safety switch, use the following procedures to check the seatbelt interlock system.

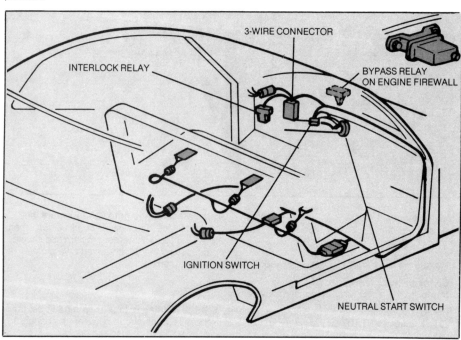

3-WIRE CONNECTOR

INTERLOCK RELAY

BYPASS RELAY
ON ENGINE FIREWALL

IGNITION SWITCH

NEUTRAL START SWITCH

1 Press and release the button on the interlock bypass relay that you'll find mounted on the firewall, then try to crank the starter.

2 If the starter doesn't crank, pull the bypass relay out of its connector and check for current at the D terminal (pink wire) of the connector with a test light. If there is no current, repair the break in the pink wire.

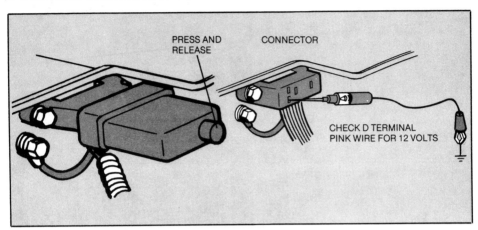

PRESS AND RELEASE

CONNECTOR

CHECK D TERMINAL PINK WIRE FOR 12 VOLTS

3 If there was current at the D terminal, connect the test light between the B terminal (green and black wire) and ground. If there is no current when the key is turned to START, repair the break in the green and black wire, plug the bypass relay back in, and try to crank the starter.

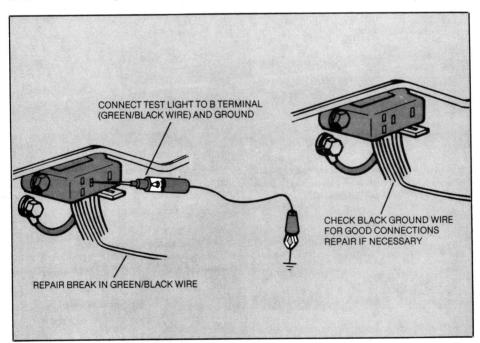

CONNECT TEST LIGHT TO B TERMINAL (GREEN/BLACK WIRE) AND GROUND

CHECK BLACK GROUND WIRE FOR GOOD CONNECTIONS REPAIR IF NECESSARY

REPAIR BREAK IN GREEN/BLACK WIRE

4 If there was current at the B terminal, check the black ground wire for good connections.

5 If the starter still won't crank, replace the bypass relay.

COMPRESSION

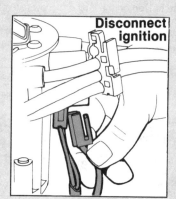
Disconnect ignition

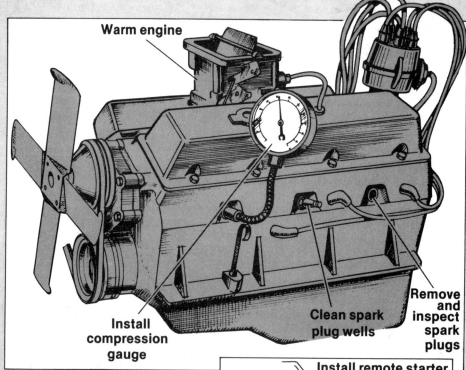
Warm engine

Install compression gauge

Clean spark plug wells

Remove and inspect spark plugs

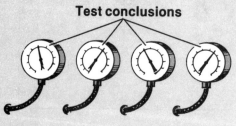
Test conclusions

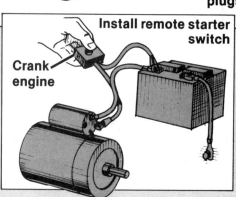
Install remote starter switch

Crank engine

5

Compression Service

PREP: Check the engine oil. If it is very old, dirty, diluted with gasoline, or not at the proper level, the compression readings may be affected. Check the battery. The starter cranks the engine during a compression test, and a weak battery can't keep the engine cranking fast enough to give accurate readings.

1 **Warm engine.** The test should be performed with the engine at normal operating temperature (at least 150°F) (p. 42).

2 **Clean spark plug wells.** This is a precaution which prevents dirt from entering the cylinders when the spark plugs are removed (p. 42).

3 **Remove and inspect spark plugs.** Remove the plugs from the cylinder head, marking them with a code to pinpoint possible problems (p. 43).

4 **Disconnect ignition.** On models with point-type ignitions, remove the coil wire from the center of the distributor cap and ground it with a jumper wire (p. 43). With HEI electronic ignition, disconnect ignition switch connector (usually a pink wire) from system.

5 **Install remote starter switch.** If you don't have a helper to crank the engine from inside the car, you'll need a remote starter switch (p. 44).

6 **Install compression gauge.** Depending on the type of gauge you have, hold it tightly against each spark plug hole or thread it into place according to the manufacturer's instructions (p. 44). Diesels require the use of a special gauge and a different procedure (see Diesel section).

7 **Crank engine and take readings.** With the throttle held open, crank the engine for four compression strokes to obtain the highest reading. Write down the cylinder number and the compression reading. Repeat the test for all cylinders (p. 45).

8 **Test conclusions.** Compare your readings with the reading for the highest cylinder. If all the readings are at least 75 percent of the highest reading and none is below about 100 psi, the compression is OK. If the readings are not OK, see "What the readings mean" (p. 45).

Essential. Basic tools • Spark plug wrench • Masking tape or clothespins • Jumper wire • Pencil and paper • Compression gauge.
Handy. Fender cover • Remote starter switch.

Danger: Hot Stuff

The compression test is performed on a warm engine. Some surfaces—the manifolds, for example—can get hotter than boiling water. So take care not to burn your hands. During the test, make sure that either the coil wire is disconnected and grounded or the electronic ignition is disconnected.

Warm up engine

CHOKE VALVE OPEN

1 Let the engine run until it reaches normal operating temperature (at least 150 °F). On cars equipped with a temperature gauge, watch the needle. On those without a temperature gauge, wait until you can kick the fast idle down to normal idle speed (see the chapter on Carburetor Service). The choke valve should be fully open.

2 Turn off the engine when operating temperature is reached.

Why test compression?

An engine compression test enables you to determine the condition of the internal parts—

valve, piston ring, and combustion-chamber sealing. Unless engine compression readings are within manufacturer's specifications, engine performance cannot be improved. If the fuel-and-air mixture is not sufficiently compressed in the cylinder, the burning will not produce all the power it should.

Clean spark plug wells

Dirt and grease that gather around the base of the spark plugs can fall into the cylinders, causing damage when you remove the plugs. Professional mechanics use compressed air to blow the dirt away.

1 Remove the spark plug cables by twisting the boots back and forth with a cable remover to free them from the plugs, and then pulling on the boot only.

2 Number each cylinder and code each cable with masking tape for easy identification when reconnecting them.

3 Brush dirt away from the spark plug wells with a brush (brushes designed for cleaning auto parts are commercially available).

4 Use lung power and a long hose (small diameter) to blow the loosened dirt away. Or if you prefer, use a bicycle tire pump.

Note: On some V-8 models, it may be difficult to use the brush on the spark plug wells. In this case using air power will be easier.

🛑 Keep the socket as straight as possible because the top of the plug is made of ceramic material and too much angle may cause it to break.

Remove and inspect spark plugs

1 Loosen the plugs using a ratchet set: a handle, an extension, a U-joint and a spark plug socket.

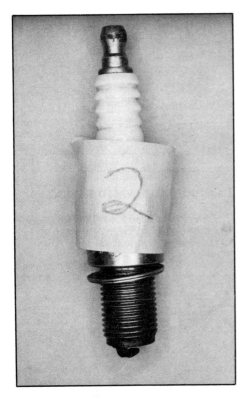

2 Carefully take out the spark plugs and mark them with the same code as the cables to pinpoint possible problems.

3 Inspect the plugs for worn or burned electrodes, improper gap, cracked ceramic insulators, and carbon or oil fouling. See the chapter on Spark Plug Service for a complete discussion of inspecting plugs.

4 Clean the plugs before reinstalling them after making the compression test.

Disconnect ignition

1 On cars with point-type ignition, remove the coil wire from the center of the distributor cap and ground it with a jumper wire. The coil wire is the one that goes between the coil and the distributor cap.

🛑 Never remove the wire from the coil's high-tension tower because the spark arcing to the coil primary side could ruin the coil.

2 On cars with HEI electronic ignition, disconnect the ignition switch feedwire connector (usually a pink wire) from the system.

3 Connect the jumper wire between the distributor side of the coil wire and any metal part of the engine.

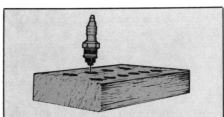

PRO SHOP You can make your own plug holder. If the spark plugs are to be reused, they should be stored in a safe place to prevent damage to the ceramic insulator or outer electrode. You can put them in a drilled block of wood, an egg carton, or push them into a piece of heavy cardboard.

Install remote starter switch

Hook up a remote starter switch if you don't have a helper to crank the engine from inside the car. Following the instructions that come with the switch, connect it between the large terminal and the small terminal on the starter solenoid. Be certain the transmission is in Neutral or Park, and set the parking brake. For a more detailed description of the hookup, see the chapter on Starting System Service.

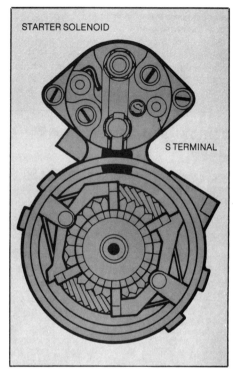

STARTER SOLENOID

S TERMINAL

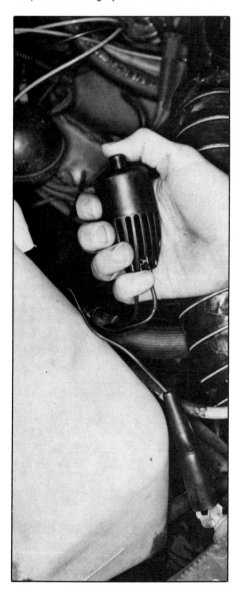

Install compression gauge

1 Open the carburetor throttle. Your helper can do this by pressing the accelerator pedal to the floor. The pedal can also be held down with a brick or similar object.

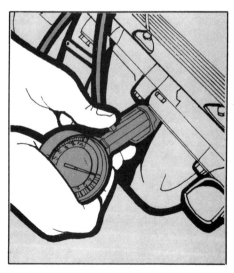

2 Install the compression gauge following the manufacturer's instructions. There are two types of gauges. The more expensive type screws into the spark plug hole. The other type has a tapered rubber plug on the end and is held over the spark plug hole by hand.

Crank engine and take readings

To record the readings for comparison later, have a pencil and pad ready. Draw a chart of the engine's cylinder layout to record the corresponding readings.

1 With the gauge in place, crank the engine for at least four compression strokes (about two or three seconds) to obtain the highest reading.

2 Record the cylinder number and reading.

3 Repeat the test for all cylinders.

🛑 Do not pump the pedal during the test or gasoline will get into the cylinders and wash the oil off their walls, thereby giving false readings.

Test conclusions

Compare your readings with the reading in the highest cylinder. If all the readings are at least 75 percent of the highest reading, the compression is OK. A range of between 120 and 160 psi, for example, is within acceptable limits for many GM engines, although as long as no cylinder is below 100 psi, the engine is probably OK. Good compression means that the piston rings, valves, and gaskets are mechanically capable of compressing the fuel-and-air mixture. If the readings are not within specs, see "What the readings mean."

What the readings mean

If one or more cylinders reads low when compared with the others, squirt a tablespoonful of engine oil into the spark plug hole. Then crank the engine again and recheck the compression. If it is now considerably higher, the piston rings may be worn. If the compression doesn't improve very much, you may have a burned or sticking valve or a blown head gasket.

If two cylinders next to each other show readings of more than 25 psi lower than the others, the head gasket is probably bad, allowing compression to pass between the cylinders.

If all the cylinders read exceptionally high, then it's likely there are excessive carbon deposits inside the combustion chamber. To confirm this, warm up the engine, ground the distributor wire from the ignition coil, and then crank the engine. If it attempts to start, then carbon may be the problem.

VACUUM

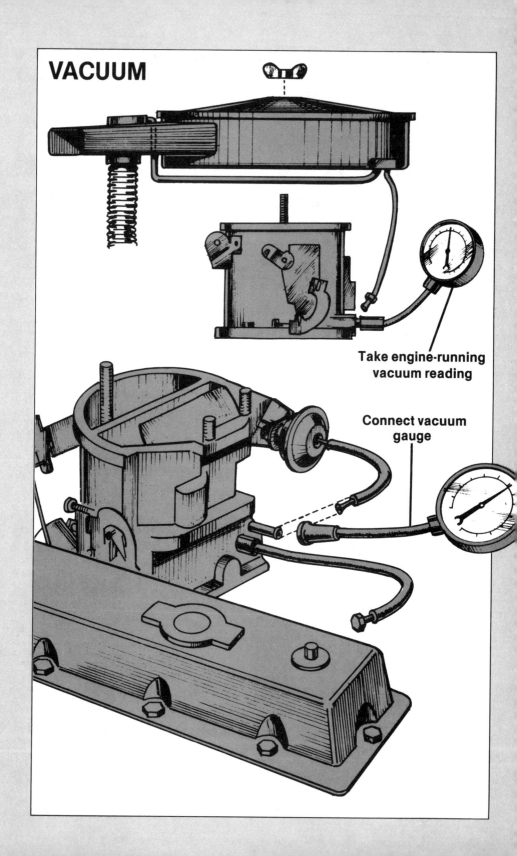

Take engine-running
vacuum reading

Connect vacuum
gauge

6

Vacuum Test

PREP: Warm the engine. It should be at normal operating temperature (at least 150° F). Check the oil. It should be at the proper level and in good condition to properly seal the rings.

1 **Connect vacuum gauge.** The gauge is attached to a source of manifold vacuum. See sources of manifold vacuum (p. 48).

2 **Take engine-running vacuum reading.** Record this reading (p. 49).

ABOUT VACUUM TESTING. The internal combustion engine is basically a vacuum pump. That is, it evacuates its cylinders to a point below atmospheric pressure so that the weight of the atmosphere rushes in to fill the void. Measuring the amount of negative pressure an engine can generate can be a valuable diagnostic tool because it provides information on the condition of the rings and valves and the sealing of the combustion chamber and intake manifold. **NOTE:** Most emission-controlled engines idle with the carburetor throttle plate open wider than on pre-controlled models. This reduces restriction and lowers the normal vacuum reading. Many gauges have calibrations that are applicable only to older models. Do not conclude that ignition or valve timing is late on the basis of these indications.

Connect vacuum gauge

Attach the vacuum gauge to a source of intake manifold vacuum, following the gauge manufacturer's instructions. All models have at least one of the two following sources of intake manifold vacuum. Hook up the gauge to the most accessible one.

The choke vacuum pulloff, sometimes called the vacuum kick, is a chamber mounted on the side of the carburetor that opens the choke slightly when actuated by intake-manifold vacuum. Trace the rubber hose between the choke vacuum pulloff nipple and the vacuum source, remove the hose, and connect the gauge to the source.

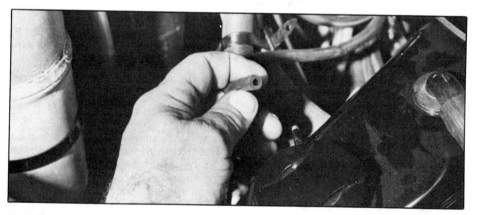

The heated-air intake system is a flapper-type valve mounted in the snorkel of the air cleaner. This also is operated by intake manifold vacuum. Trace the rubber hose connected to the valve back to the thermostatic bleed valve in the air cleaner and from there down to the manifold vacuum source. Disconnect the hose and attach the vacuum gauge to the source.

Take engine-running vacuum reading

A high, steady vacuum reading (between 14 and 22 inches of vacuum depending on the engine) as the engine idles tells you that you have a mechanically sound engine, good rings, valves, valve guides, a properly sealed combustion chamber and intake manifold, and correct valve and ignition timing.

Note: Acceptable vacuum readings vary because the design characteristics of different engines vary. For example, if your car has a high-performance engine with a ''hot'' camshaft, readings will be lower than normal even though all internal engine parts may be in excellent condition. Also, recent emission-controlled engines idle with the throttle plate in a more open position than older engines, so the idle vacuum is lower.

1 Take the engine-running vacuum reading with the vacuum gauge connected.

2 Record the reading and compare it with ''What the readings mean.''

3 Shut off the engine.

What the readings mean

If the reading is steady but considerably lower than normal, the problem may be nothing more serious than late ignition timing. Check this with a timing light. But your engine could have worn piston rings (check for this by performing a compression test) or late valve timing.

If the reading is steady and very low, suspect a vacuum leak at the intake manifold or carburetor mounting gaskets, or in a vacuum hose to an accessory.

If the needle moves regularly between a high and a low reading, a leaking head gasket might be the problem.

An intermittent fluctuation of the needle can be caused by an ignition problem or a sticking valve.

If, when the rpm is raised above idle and held there, and the reading drops slowly to a very low point, the exhaust system may be restricted. One possibility is a clogged catalytic converter on 1975 and newer models.

If the needle floats slowly over about a five-point range, the carburetor mixture may be out of adjustment. Another possibility is a minor vacuum leak.

Note: When you find your engine has low or uneven vacuum, make a compression test if you haven't already made one. You cannot successfully tune your engine until poor compression or vacuum leaks are corrected.

How to correct a vacuum leak

If a vacuum leak is suspected, follow this procedure to locate and correct the problem.

1 Check all vacuum hoses to make sure they are connected or plugged.

2 Feel the vacuum hose(s). It should be soft and pliable. Also look for cracked vacuum hose(s). Vacuum hoses become brittle with age and can leak. If the vacuum hose is cracked or leaky, replace it and retest.

3 If vacuum leak is still present, it may be in the intake manifold or carburetor mounting gasket. To check this, start engine and run at idle speed. Spray penetrating oil on both the intake manifold sealing surface and the carburetor sealing surface. If engine rpm increases while spraying, one of these gaskets may be at fault. Have it checked by a professional mechanic.

DISTRIBUTOR

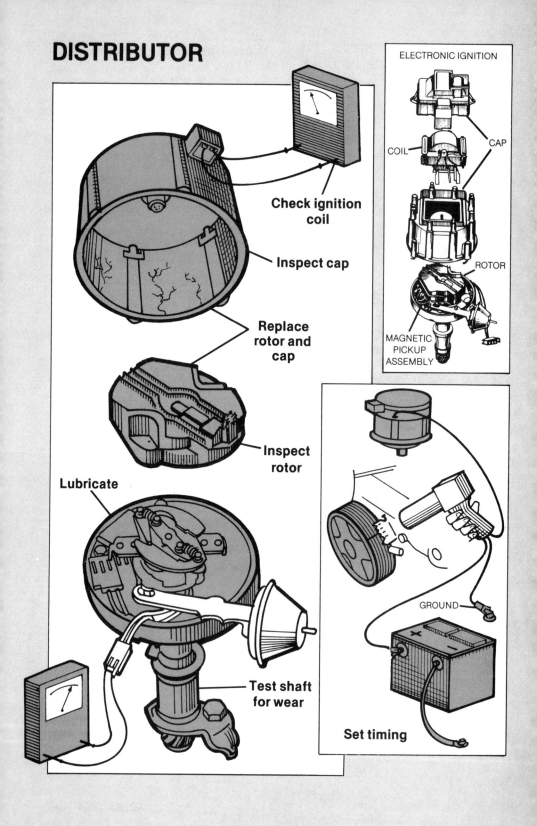

ELECTRONIC IGNITION

COIL

CAP

ROTOR

MAGNETIC PICKUP ASSEMBLY

Check ignition coil

Inspect cap

Replace rotor and cap

Inspect rotor

Lubricate

Test shaft for wear

GROUND

Set timing

7

Distributor Service

1 **Remove and inspect cap.** Look for cracks and burned terminals. Remove the cables and inspect the towers (p. 52).

2 **Remove and inspect rotor.** Look for cracks, corrosion, and burns (p. 53). If your car is equipped with electronic ignition, proceed to step 9.

3 **Inspect points.** If they are pitted or burned, or if the rubbing block is worn, replace them. Replace the condenser when replacing the points (p. 53).

4 **Clean distributor housing.** Wipe the breaker plate and cam clean. Check the cam for excessive movement (p. 54).

5 **Lubricate distributor.** Apply a light coating of cam lube to the cam. Apply a drop of light oil to the distributor lubrication locations (p. 54).

6 **Install new points.** Position the points on the breaker plate. On internal-adjustment distributors, tighten the holding screw finger-tight. On external-adjustment "window" distributors, tighten the screws all the way (p. 54).

7 **Find high spot on cam lobe.** Install a remote starter switch (p. 55) or have a helper crank the engine.

8 **Set point gap.** Adjust the gap with a feeler gauge and tighten the holding screw on internal-adjustment distributors. On external-adjustment "window" distributors, set the point gap to the proper feeler-gauge width with an Allen wrench (p. 55).

9 **Test shaft for wear.** Push the distributor shaft from side to side. If the point gap changes, the distributor is worn. On electronic ignitions, a worn distributor may cause the gap between the magnetic pickup core and the armature to decrease or close up completely (p. 56).

10 **Replace rotor and distributor cap.** Make sure the rotor is properly seated. Position the cap correctly and fasten it to the distributor (p. 57).

11 **Check dwell.** Measure the point gap with a dwell meter (p. 57). On cars with electronic ignitions, dwell is not adjustable. Proceed to step 12.

12 **Set timing.** Connect a timing light to the number 1 spark plug wire, remove and plug distributor vacuum line(s), and set the timing (p. 58). Reconnect the vacuum line and check the vacuum advance (p. 59).

13 **Test resistor wire.** This can easily be done with a test light (p. 60).

14 **Check ignition coil.** Clean the coil tower when servicing the distributor (p. 60). Replace the coil if it is damaged.

Essential. Basic tools • Towels or clean rags • Cam lube • Light oil • Feeler gauge • Timing light • Distributor wrench • Flashlight • 1/8-inch Allen wrench for "window" distributors • Volt/Ohmmeter.
Handy. Remote starter switch • Tach/dwell meter • Magnetic screwdriver • 12-volt test light.

Remove and inspect cap

1 Disconnect the battery ground cable to avoid the possibility of accidental shorts.

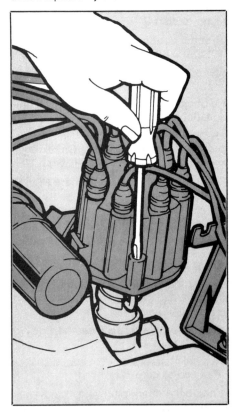

2 Unfasten the cap from the distributor.
The cap is secured with two screws or two L-shaped, spring-loaded hooks with screw heads. Using a screwdriver, press down on the hook screw heads and rotate a quarter of a

turn in either direction to release the cap.

3 Inspect the cap with a flashlight. Check the inside and outside for cracks, carbon tracks, broken towers, and burned terminals. If you find any such conditions, replace the cap. Minute cracks or carbon tracking can cause an engine to miss. Look at the center electrode to make sure it hasn't worn away.

4 Carefully remove the spark plug wires one at a time from the top of the cap and clean and inspect them.
CAUTION: Never pull just on the wire. Twist the boot one-half turn in each direction to free it from the cap, making sure the wire end also turns.

With electronic ignition, unsnap the two plastic latches at the top of the cap and remove the plastic retaining ring and plug wires. Both the cap and the wire ends should be free of corrosion. You should clean or replace them if they are not. A bad cap can cause hard starting, engine misfiring, or prevent starting altogether.

5 Reinsert each wire back in its hole.
🛑 Don't mix up the wires. If you do, you will have to follow the procedure in the following PRO SHOP.

PRO SHOP Here's how to restore the correct firing order should you get the plug wires mixed up. First, find out the firing order for your engine. It may be stamped on the intake manifold. Pontiac 4s have a 1-3-4-2 firing order, inline 6s a 1-5-3-6-2-4 order, V-6s a 1-6-5-4-3-2 order, and V-8s a 1-8-4-3-6-5-7-2 order. You must also know the direction in which the distributor rotor rotates—this can be determined by cranking the engine with the distributor cap off.

Then ascertain the position of each cylinder. On inline 6s, cylinders are numbered 1 to 6 in order from front to rear. V-8s have cylinders numbered 1-3-5-7 from front to rear on the left (driver's side) bank, and 2-4-6-8 on the right bank. V-6 cylinders are numbered 1-3-5 on the left bank and 2-4-6 on the right bank.

Finally, find the number 1 wire's position in the cap. Do this by removing number 1 spark plug, placing your finger over the plug hole, and cranking the engine in bursts. When you feel compression, continue cranking slowly until the timing marks line up. Note the position of the rotor. The corresponding contact on the cap is the number 1 wire's position. Working in the direction of rotor rotation from there, plug each wire into its hole according to the correct firing order.

Remove and inspect rotor

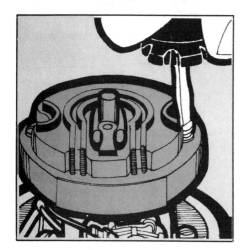

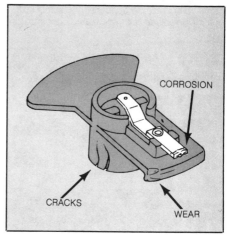

On some models, the rotor is attached to the distributor shaft with two screws which must be unscrewed to remove the rotor on V8s and V6s. On other models, the rotor is removed simply by pulling it straight up. Inspect the rotor for cracks, chips, corrosion, burns, or weak contact spring tension. Turn it over and inspect the underside with a flashlight for electrical tracking (indicated by black lines on the surface). You should replace a rotor with any of the above conditions.

When reinstalling the rotor, make sure you line it up properly on the shaft. On the screw-on type, there is one round and one square protrusion on the bottom that fit into corresponding holes at the top of the shaft. The push-on type has a square positioning block inside that must slip into the corresponding notch at the top of the shaft. Make sure the rotor is pushed down all the way.

Note: Always replace the cap and rotor in pairs. If your car is equipped with electronic ignition, proceed to "Test shaft for wear."

Remove and inspect points

1 Inspect the point contacts for wear. If they are light gray and have a smooth surface, they can be reused.

2 Replace the points if they are pitted, worn, loose, or blue in color, or if the rubbing block is worn or the pivot point damaged. If you replace the points, also replace the condenser. Note the position of the old condenser in the hold-down clip before removing the screw. Position the new condenser in the same place. On some point sets, the condenser is built in so you must replace both points and condenser as a unit.

3 To remove the points, take out the wires that are attached to them.

4 Remove the retaining screw(s) from the base of the points with a magnetic screwdriver. (On V-8s the screws do not have to be removed.) Be careful not to drop screws into the distributor.

Clean distributor housing

1 Wipe the breaker plate and cam clean of dirt and old cam lube with a clean towel or rag.

2 Check the cam lobes for roughness or pitting. If the cam is rough, the points will not stay in adjustment.

3 Also check the sideplay of the distributor shaft by moving it from side to side. If the shaft is not snug, the distributor will probably have to be replaced. Have it checked out by a professional mechanic.

Lubricate distributor

1 Apply a light coating of cam lube to the distributor cam.

Note: Electronic ignition distributors don't have a cam, so they don't require lube. Spread not more than two match-heads worth of lube

equally around the cam, then wipe off any excess.

2 Apply a drop of light oil to the advance weight pivot points.

3 Rotate the cam wiper mounted on the breaker plate 180 degrees, if your car is so equipped. If the wiper has dried out, lubricate or replace it.

Install new points

1 Place the points on the distributor breaker plate and tighten the holding screw finger-tight on an internal-adjustment distributor. Tighten each hold-down screw all the way on an external-adjustment "window" distributor.

🛑 Be sure the wire terminals are installed on top of the point set, not under it. Incorrect installation can change the angle of the points. Make sure the point set sits flat, and be careful that no grease or dirt gets on the point surfaces.

2 Install a new condenser. If the new point set has an integral condenser, skip this step.

3 Reconnect the primary and condenser wires to the point set.

🛑 Make sure the wires don't touch the

breaker plate or the distributor base, or rub on the cam or the breaker plate. If they do, a short circuit may result and the car won't start.

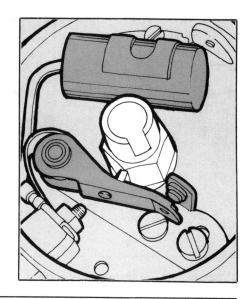

Find high spot on cam lobe

1 **Position the distributor cam** so one of its high spots is against the point rubbing block.

2 **Crank the engine with a remote starter switch** (see the chapter on Starting System Service) or have a helper crank the engine in short bursts until the high spot of the cam is in position. The high spot is where the points are open widest.

Set point gap

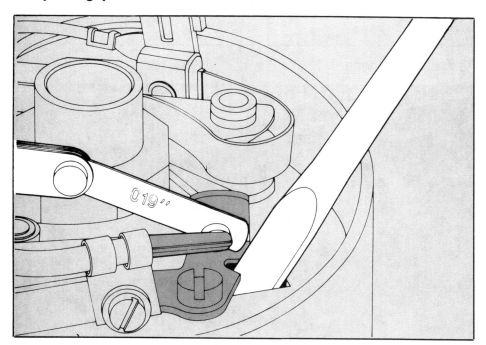

1 **Measure the gap** between the two point faces with a clean feeler gauge.

2 **Adjust the gap** until it meets the specifications on the underhood label (usually .019 inch). On an internal-adjustment distributor, the gap is changed by moving the base of the point set toward or away from the distributor cam. Insert a screwdriver blade into the adjustment slot. Make sure the points are open the widest at the high spot of the cam and closed on the flat spot. Otherwise the engine will not start.

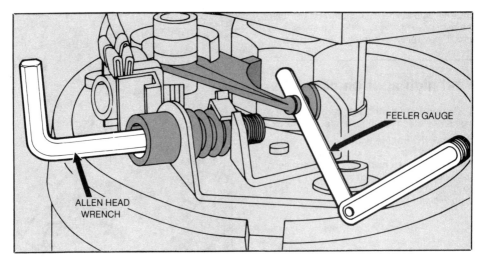

FEELER GAUGE

ALLEN HEAD
WRENCH

3 Tighten the point screw when the gap is correct.

4 Recheck the gap to make sure it hasn't moved. Do this by cranking the engine and remeasuring the gap after you make sure one of the cam's high spots is against the point rubbing block.

OR if your car is equipped with an external-adjustment "window" distributor, simply turn the screw that spreads the points in or out with an Allen wrench until the gap is correct with the rubbing block on the high spot of the cam.

Test shaft for wear

1 Push the distributor shaft in the direction of the rubbing block. If the point gap changes, the distributor is worn and should be repaired or replaced. If your car has electronic ignition, a worn shaft may allow the gap between the

magnetic pickup core and the armature to decrease or close up completely.

2 Have the distributor checked out by a professional mechanic before replacing it.

Replace rotor and distributor cap

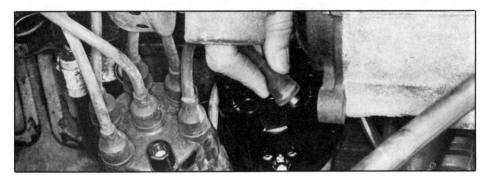

To replace a push-on type rotor, fit its locating tab into the locating slot on the distributor shaft. Be sure the rotor is properly seated. To replace a screw-on type rotor, make sure the square and round protrusions on the bottom of the rotor go into the matching holes at the top of the distributor shaft.

1 Unfasten the old cap from the distributor but leave the wires connected.

2 Hold the new cap next to the old cap and install each wire into its same relative hole in the new cap. If you replace only one wire at a time, you can easily avoid getting the wires into the wrong cap holes and disrupting the firing order.

OR if your car is equipped with electronic ignition, unsnap the two plastic latches and remove the wires and their plastic retaining ring. Also, some electronic ignition distributor caps have the coil mounted on them. Remove it from the old cap and reinstall it on the new one.

3 Place the new cap on the distributor in the same relative position as the old one after all the wires have been installed.

4 Now line up the locating slot on the distributor base with the corresponding slot on the cap.

5 Fasten the cap by turning the retaining screws or turning the latches until they catch under the distributor body.

Note: If your car is equipped with electronic ignition, proceed to "Set timing," since dwell is not adjustable on electronic ignitions.

Check dwell

1 Attach a dwell meter according to the manufacturer's instructions.

2 Start the car and observe the reading. If it is within the specifications on the underhood label (usually 32° on a 6-cylinder, 30° on a V-8), proceed to the next step. If the dwell is off, the point gap must be reset. The smaller the gap, the larger the dwell reading.

PRO SHOP Here's a tip on setting dwell on external-adjustment "window" distributors. Simply open the sliding metal door on the cap, insert an Allen wrench into the adjusting screw, and turn until the meter reads the correct dwell (usually 30° on a V-8). If you don't have a dwell-meter, turn the screw inward (clockwise) until the engine misfires, then back off one-half turn. Remember, the smaller the gap, the larger the dwell. Also, dwell affects timing—the larger the dwell, the later the spark. That's why spark retards as the rubbing block wears.

About dwell meters

A dwell meter electronically determines how long the points remain closed and converts that information into the number of degrees the distributor turns. The point gap directly affects dwell. A dwell reading greater than specifications means the point gap is too narrow, and the space between the points needs to be opened up. A dwell reading less than specs means the point gap is too wide and the space between the points must be lessened. Correct dwell is important for ignition system performance. If the dwell is too short, the coil won't produce as "hot" a spark as it should. Also, as the rubbing block wears, gap decreases and that retards timing.

A dwell meter has two wires. One is hooked up to the coil at the primary terminal marked (neg), (−) or (Dist). The other wire is connected to a ground such as the negative terminal of the battery or a metal part on the engine, such as a manifold bolt. Once the wires are hooked up, select the proper scale which indicates the number of cylinders your car's engine has. Start the car and observe the needle. A good dwell reading is within engine specs and the needle is steady while the car is being accelerated from idle to high speed.

Set timing

Ignition timing is one of the most important adjustments you can make on your engine to improve performance and gas mileage. Timing is adjusted so the spark occurs a specified number of degrees before top dead center (BTDC) or after top dead center (ATDC) of the compression stroke. Top dead center is the highest point of piston travel in the cylinder. Both mechanical (centrifugal) and vacuum spark advances are based on the specified timing adjustment. If the initial timing position is off, all the subsequent timing adjustments that are made automatically by the distributor will also be off.

1 Wipe the timing marks clean and apply a dab of white paint to the notch of the vibration damper or pulley and the correct timing setting mark on the indicator. Use the timing specs on the EPA (Environmental Protection Agency) sticker that is in your car's engine compartment, if it's still readable. The sticker gives you the basic timing specs and the exact setting procedure. The proper idle speed is also specified. Timing is usually set on a warm engine at idle.

2 Tag and remove the vacuum hose from the distributor.

3 Plug the end of the hose with a pencil or golf tee.

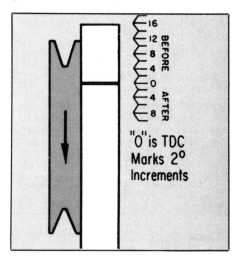

"0" is TDC
Marks 2° Increments

4 Connect a timing light to the engine, following the manufacturer's instructions. A typical timing light has three leads. One is connected to the positive (+) terminal of the battery, one is connected to the negative (−) terminal or a ground, and one is connected to the number 1 spark plug wire. The number 1 cylinder on 6-cylinder inline engines is the front cylinder, and on V-6 and V-8 engines it is the front cylinder on the left (driver's side) bank.

5 Next, connect a tachometer to the engine, following the manufacturer's instructions. A typical tach has two leads. One is connected to a ground, such as the negative battery terminal. The other is connected to the distributor side of the coil. This lead is usually marked (−) or (Dist).

6 Start the engine and allow it to reach nor-

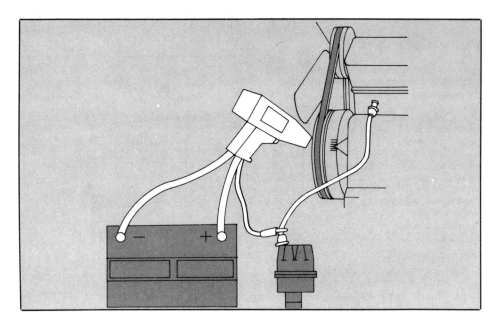

mal operating temperature (at least 150 °F).

7 Check the tach for correct engine rpm and aim the timing light at the timing marks. They should line up.
CAUTION: Be extremely careful not to get the timing light, its wires or your fingers near the fan, the belts, or the pulleys.

8 If the timing is not within specs, loosen the distributor hold-down bolt (usually 1/2 or 9/16 inch) and rotate the distributor as necessary to align the proper timing mark with the notch.

STOP You may have to slow down the idle speed in order to make sure the distributor is not advancing.

9 When the timing is set, tighten the distributor hold-down bolt.

10 Reset the idle speed if it was previously altered.

11 Reattach the vacuum hose you removed in step 3.

12 Make a quick check of the vacuum advance. With the timing light pointed at the timing marks, briefly accelerate the engine. If the timing mark on the crankshaft pulley moves off the scale as the engine accelerates, then the vacuum advance is working properly. If the timing mark does not advance, a defective vacuum advance unit or vacuum supply line is the likely cause. You should see a pro.

Note: On certain models and years, the vacuum advance operates only after the engine warms up or when the transmission is in high gear or when a certain rpm is reached. On these models, you will not be able to check the vacuum advance yourself. The job must be performed by a pro.

13 Shut off the engine and remove the timing light.

PRO SHOP If you remove and reinstall the distributor, you must make sure you get it back properly engaged with its driving gear or the timing will be way off. Remove the cap and *carefully* note the position of the rotor. See exactly where the contact on the rotor is pointing and mark the spot on the block, rocker cover, etc.

Note the orientation of the vacuum advance unit, remove the distributor hold-down bolt, and pull the distributor out of the engine. Do not crank the engine while the distributor is out of the car.

To reinstall the distributor, insert it into its hole. Make sure the oil pump drive shaft engages the socket in the bottom of the shaft. The rotor will turn as its drive gears mesh. Be sure the rotor is pointing precisely at the mark when the distributor is down all the way. You may have to pull it out and move it one tooth in either direction to accomplish this. Rotate the distributor until the vacuum advance unit is in its former position, then reinstall and tighten the hold-down bolt. Finally, reset the timing.

Test resistor wire

Most cars have a device called a ballast resistor which limits the amount of current that goes to the ignition system, thus increasing distributor point life. GM cars have what is called an internal ballast resistor, which is actually a high-resistance wire built into the wiring harness between the ignition switch and the positive terminal of the ignition coil. A car with a bad ballast resistor will fire with the key in the START position and the engine turning over. But when the key is returned to the ON position, the engine will stall. The easiest way to check a ballast resistor is with a test light.

Note: Electronic HEI (High Energy Ignition) systems used on all 1975 and newer models have no ballast resistor.

1 To check the resistor wire, hook up one lead of a 12-volt test light to a ground (such as the negative (−) terminal of the battery) and the other lead to the positive (+) or (BAT) side of the ignition coil. The battery side of the ignition coil is the side that does not go to the distributor.

2 The bulb should light with the ignition key in the ON position. If it does not, there is a defect in the wiring or in the ignition switch.

Check ignition coil

The ignition coil transforms low battery voltage into high. While there is no prescribed maintenance for a coil, you can help keep it efficient by cleaning dirt off the tower when you service the distributor.

Note: Some electronic HEI distributors have an integrated coil mounted in the cap, so there is no coil tower.

1 Remove the high-tension wire from the center of the coil, wipe the top, and clean out the hole inside the tower.

2 Inspect the top for electrical tracking between the center tower and the positive (+) and negative (−) terminals.

3 Replace the coil if it is physically damaged or if there is evidence of tracking.

4 Make sure the positive and negative wires are securely attached after you have reinstalled an old coil or installed a new one.

To check coil on breaker-point ignition systems

If your car won't start, and the fuel system and the rest of the ignition system check out, test the coil.

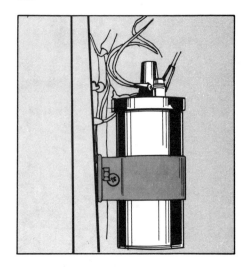

A good quick-check is to remove the cap, crank the engine until the points are closed, then leave the key in the ON position. Now, pull the coil wire out of its socket in the middle of the distributor cap, leaving the other end in the coil tower. Using an insulated tool to avoid a shock, hold the free end of the coil wire about 3/8 inch away from a clean metal surface of the engine and open the points with an insulated screwdriver. You should see a strong spark at the coil wire. If not, run a jumper wire from the positive (+) terminal of the battery to the BAT or positive terminal of the coil and try again. If there's a spark now, the coil is not faulty.

To replace ignition coil

1 To remove the ignition coil, disconnect the wires from their terminals and mark them for easy reinstallation.

2 Carefully grasp the rubber boot of the coil tower cable and twist it gently to the left and right.

3 Ease the cable out of the coil tower by holding the boot between your fingers. Don't pull or yank on the cable itself.

4 Now remove the coil from its bracket or remove the bracket itself.

5 To install the new coil, insert it into the bracket and tighten the bracket.

6 Hook up the wires to their correct terminals. The wire from the ignition switch and ballast resistor is connected to the terminal marked (BAT) or (+). The wire going to the distributor is connected to the terminal marked (DIST) or (−).

Testing and servicing electronic ignitions

All 1975 and newer models have electronic HEI (High Energy Ignition) systems in which the points and condenser have been replaced by a timer core and polepiece pickup assembly. It is installed where the distributor cam and breaker set would be in a conventional system. The distributor cap and rotor in both systems are serviced in basically the same way. In cases of electronic ignition system failure, however, the problem is usually hard to track down. You'll need a volt/ohmmeter and some patience to find out whether the magnetic pickup (stator), the electronic control module, or the wiring is at fault. The pickup coil and the electronic control module can be replaced by a do-it-yourselfer. Here is a step-by-step photo sequence on service and testing procedures for the electronic ignition system in your car.

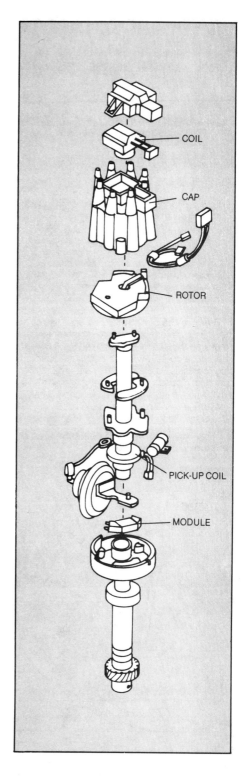

COIL

CAP

ROTOR

PICK-UP COIL

MODULE

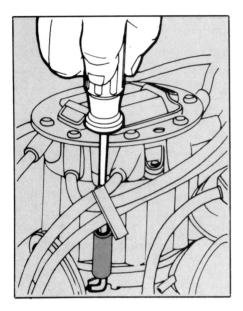

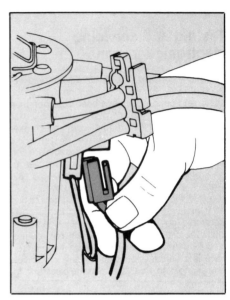

1 Remove the distributor cap and inspect the underside for arcing across the terminals, cracks on the side of the cap, and signs of rotor blade contact with the distributor spark plug terminals. Make sure the center carbon button is in good working order. It should move down when pressure is put on it and up when pressure is released. Replace the cap if necessary. Also check the plug wires.

2 Wipe away any signs of contamination or moisture with a clean cloth.

3 Inspect the rotor blade and spring contact for wear, burns, and breaks. Replace the rotor, if necessary.

4 Disconnect the distributor wire harness connector. Inspect both sides for corrosion, broken leads, and shorting.

5 Make sure the timer core (the part that rotates) is not making contact with the pole-piece (pickup coil).

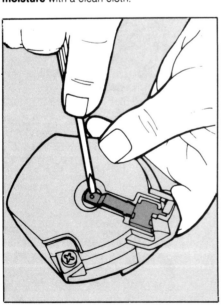

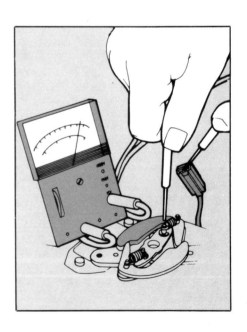

6 In a no-start situation, remove a spark plug wire and use an insulated tool to hold it 1/4 inch from a good ground while a helper cranks the engine. If there is a strong spark, the trouble is probably not in the ignition system. If there is no spark, proceed to step 7.

7 If there is no spark or only a very weak spark, use a voltmeter to check for current feed to the BAT terminal on the distributor cap (in systems with integral coil) or on the coil (in systems with external coil). Attach the negative lead of the voltmeter to a good ground and touch the positive lead to the BAT terminal. You should read battery voltage with the ignition switch on. If you do not have a voltmeter, you can use a test light. If there is no voltage reading, there is an open in the circuit running from the battery through the ignition switch to the BAT terminal. If there is a voltage reading, proceed to the next step.

8 On integral coil systems, remove the cap and unplug its wire connector. Using an ohm-meter, check resistance between the BAT and TACH terminals on the cap. This tests coil primary winding resistance. If the reading is above one ohm, replace the coil. If it is less than one ohm, go to step 10.

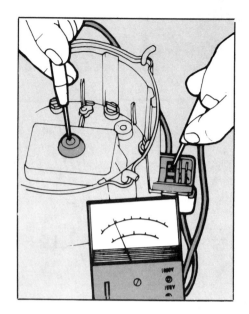

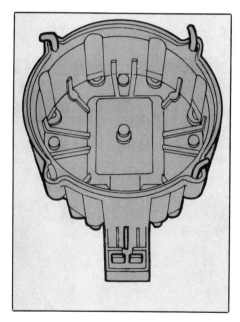

9 On external coil systems, disconnect the two primary lead wires from the coil and attach an ohmmeter between the primary terminals on the coil. If the reading is above one ohm, replace the coil. If it is less than one ohm, go to Step 11.

10 On integral coil systems, check coil secondary resistance by touching the ohm-meter leads to the TACH terminal and the carbon contact in the center of the underside of the cap. The reading should be 6000 to 30,000 ohms. Then touch the ohmmeter leads to the carbon contact and the ground terminal of the cap (between the BAT and TACH terminals). The reading should be in the above range. If either reading is above or below that range, replace the coil. If both readings are OK, go to step 12.

11 On external coil systems, check coil secondary resistance by touching the ohm-meter leads to one of the coil primary terminals and the secondary terminal (the one the high-tension wire is attached to). The reading should be 6000 to 30,000 ohms. If it is not, replace the coil. Touch the ohmmeter leads to a primary terminal and a ground terminal (one of the four screw heads). The reading should be infinite (no continuity). If it is not, replace the coil. If both readings are OK, go on to the next step.

12 With either integral or external coil systems, check the pickup coil by removing its two wires from the electronic control module, then touch one lead of the ohmmeter to either wire and the other lead to ground. The reading should be infinite (no continuity). If you get a reading, replace the pickup coil. If there's no reading, go to the next step.

13 Connect the ohmmeter leads to the two pickup coil wires. The reading should be between 500 and 1500 ohms. If it is not, replace the pickup coil.

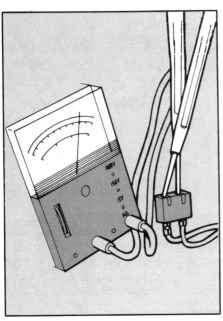

14 **If the system has passed all the above tests,** but there is still no spark, replace the electronic control module.

To replace coil in integral coil systems

1 **Disconnect the battery wire and harness connector** from the distributor cap.

2 **Remove the three screws** holding the coil cover to the distributor cap.

3 **Remove the four screws** holding the coil to the cap.

4 **Remove the ground wire** from the coil, then push the leads from under the connectors and remove the coil.

5 **Push the lead wires** of the new coil into the connector on the side of the cap—the black wire to the center terminal, the brown next to the vacuum advance unit, the pink opposite the vacuum advance unit.

6 **Install the coil hold-down screws,** placing the ground wire under one screw. Then install the coil cover and screws.

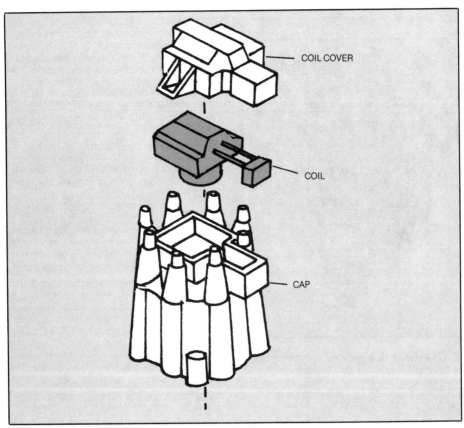

COIL COVER

COIL

CAP

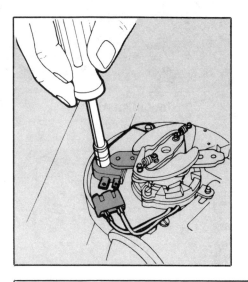

To replace electronic control module

1 Remove the rotor.

2 **Remove the two module hold-down screws,** the module connector, and the two pickup coil leads, noting their positions. Then lift out the module.

3 **Apply a liberal coating** of special silicone grease to the metal surface where the module will be mounted.

Do not skip this step or else the new module will overheat. Grease is supplied with the new module.

4 **Reattach the wiring** to the new module, screw it down, and install the rotor.

ECONOTIP Tampering refers to changing the design of or adjustments on an engine. It includes removal of emission-control devices, blocking of hoses, disconnecting wires, or adjusting timing and mixture controls outside of factory specifications. Tampering is against federal law for any commercial auto repair establishment. It is not against the law for an individual car owner to tamper with his car, however.

The Environmental Protection Agency (EPA) did a study of tampering and its effect on gas mileage. The study was done on a very small number of cars, but it showed that the average gas mileage after tampering was 3½ percent worse. However, one car showed a 9.9 percent improvement after tampering. All the cars were then taken to the EPA technicians for scientific tampering. The result was an average 7 percent improvement.

The answer about tampering is that an automotive engineer can do it and improve gas mileage. A repair shop can do it successfully only a small percentage of the time, but it is illegal for them to do it anyway. So the chances that a do-it-youselfer can improve mileage by tampering are not good. Instead, it will probably make the mileage worse.

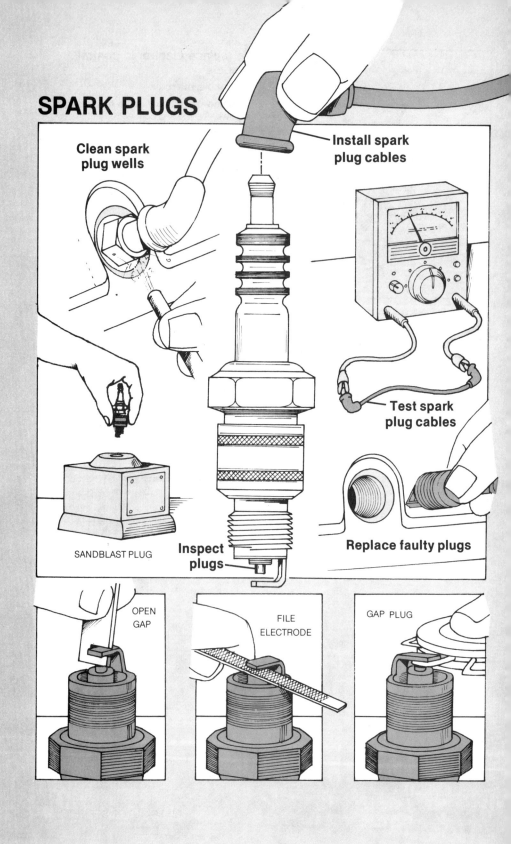

SPARK PLUGS

Clean spark plug wells

Install spark plug cables

Test spark plug cables

SANDBLAST PLUG

Inspect plugs

Replace faulty plugs

OPEN GAP

FILE ELECTRODE

GAP PLUG

8

Spark Plug Service

1 **Clean spark plug wells.** This is a precaution which prevents dirt from entering the cylinders when the spark plugs are removed (p. 68).

2 **Remove and inspect plugs.** Check the plugs for cracks, compression leaks, electrode wear, and oil or carbon deposits. For especially hard-to-remove plugs, use penetrating oil (p. 68).

3 **Service reusable plugs.** Clean them with a sandblaster. Open the plug gap and file the electrode square. Gap the plugs and reinstall them (p. 69).

4 **Replace faulty plugs.** Make sure the new plugs have the correct heat range and the same thread reach and seat design as the ones you removed. Also, gap the new plugs to meet your car's specs. Screw in the plugs by hand until they are finger-tight. Then tighten them with a wrench (p. 72).

5 **Inspect and test spark plug cables.** Check them for cuts, punctures, cracks, and age. Test them for resistance. Damaged or old cables can cause missing and poor engine performance and gas mileage, as well as hard starting in wet weather (p. 73).

6 **Install spark plug cables.** Make sure the cables are of the correct length and are routed properly (p. 75).

Essential. Basic tools • Spark plug socket wrench • Extension • Spark plug cleaning solvent • Stiff brush • File • Wire feeler gauge • Towels or clean rags • Oil • Ohmmeter • Jumper wire.
Handy. Masking tape and/or spring clothespin • Spark plug cable remover • Sandblaster (plug cleaner) • Electrode bending tool • Torque wrench.

Clean spark plug wells

Dirt and grease that gather around the base of the spark plugs can fall into the cylinders, causing damage when you remove the plugs. Professional mechanics use compressed air to blow the dirt away. The do-it-yourselfer can use lung power and a narrow hose to achieve the same purpose. For a complete illustrated description of this procedure, see the chapter on Compression Service.

Remove and inspect plugs

Identify all the spark plug cables. Before removing them, label each one, either with masking tape or a spring clothespin, so you will be able to connect the right cable to the right cylinder after you have serviced the plugs.

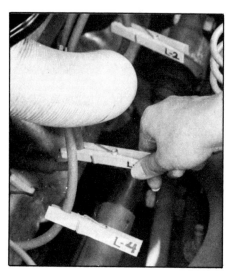

1 Mark the tape or clothespin. If you're working on a V-6 engine, the cylinders on the left bank are numbered 1-3-5 front to rear. The right bank is numbered 2-4-6 (left is the driver's side, right is the passenger's side). On a V-8, the left bank is 1-3-5-7, the right bank 2-4-6-8. On in-line engines, all you have to do is number the plug cables from front to rear.

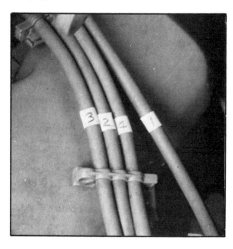

Note: Keep in mind that cables routed through a bracket on the cylinder head cover or the engine are not always in the same sequence as they appear attached to the plugs. For example, number 1 cable may be positioned third in the bracket. See "How to avoid getting caught in the crossfire" later in this chapter.

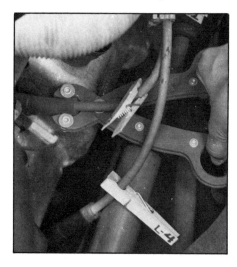

2 Remove the spark plug cables. To do this, grasp the boot—the heavy, rubbery part at the spark plug port—with a spark plug cable remover and twist the boot back and forth to free it from the plug. Pull on the boot.

If you try to remove the cables by pulling on them, you stand a good chance of breaking the electrical conductor inside. So always grab the cables by their boots.

3 If the engine is cold and you do not have a special cable remover, grasp the cable by its boot and carefully twist it back and forth to free it from the plug terminal. Then, still holding the boot, pull it carefully off the plug. Remove all the cables this way.

4 Remove the spark plugs using a spark plug wrench and, if necessary, an extension long enough to reach the plug you are removing. Place the socket over the plugs and turn the wrench counterclockwise. If they won't unscrew all the way, apply penetrating oil to the treads, screw them back in, wait a minute and try again.

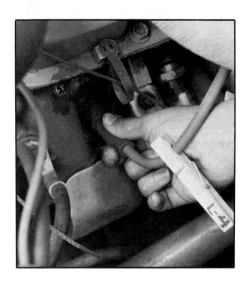

Servicing reusable plugs

If the spark plugs appear to be OK and they have been in the car for less than 10,000 miles, you can clean, file, regap, and reinstall them. If they don't show too much wear, you can simply wash them with a solvent and a stiff brush. The most important area is the ceramic nose around the center electrode. This is where shunts can form that bleed off voltage and cause misfiring. Never use a wire brush on the electrodes. This may etch them, allowing fresh deposits to adhere more easily.

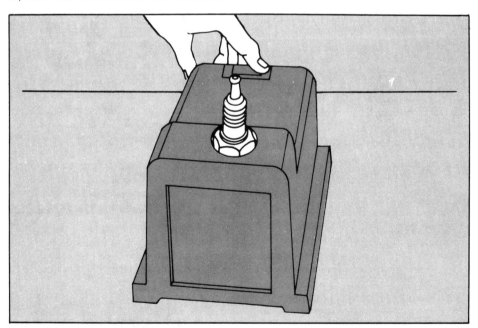

1 The best way to clean plugs is to sandblast them. If you don't have this kind of plug cleaner, for a small fee your local service shop will sandblast them.

(Continued)

Reading your plugs

Knowing how to "read" your plugs can help you do a better job tuning up your car. The 15 descriptions which follow should get you going:

1 Fluffy gray deposits: Normal for emission-controlled engines and no-lead fuel. Plug has high mileage and should be replaced.

2 Soft deposits on center and darker deposits on side electrodes: proper heat range at moderate speeds.

3 Light tan deposits on a well-used plug.

4 Soft white deposits on center electrode and insulator: Normal with regular fuel.

5 Normal fluffy brown deposits on insulator. Sooty deposits on shell suggest a rich mixture.

6 Slightly oily deposits on shell: Engine probably not fully broken in.

7 Detonation damage: Possible causes: a) over-advanced ignition timing; b) fuel too low in octane; c) EGR system malfunctioning.

8 Preignition damage: White deposits on insulator, burned electrodes: Possible causes: a) plug too hot; b) improper ignition timing; c) cooling or exhaust system clogged.

9 Sooty deposits on insulator and electrodes: Possible causes: a) excessively rich mixture due to sticking choke or defective carburetor; b) faulty primary circuit or spark plug wires.

10 Oil fouled: Possible causes: a) piston ring or valve-guide seal leakage; b) defective PCV system.

11 Carbon fouled: Possible causes: a) oil passing rings or valves; b) defective PCV system; c) spark plug too cold; d) mixture too rich.

12 Dirt fouling: Look for defective air cleaner.

13 Bridged gap: Deposits accumulated at low speed; causes dead cylinder.

14 Glazed insulator: May mean spark plug too hot.

15 Splashed insulator: Oily accumulation in cylinder breaks loose and fouls plug after tuneup.

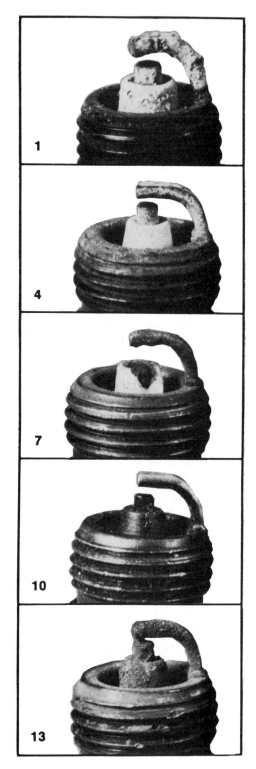

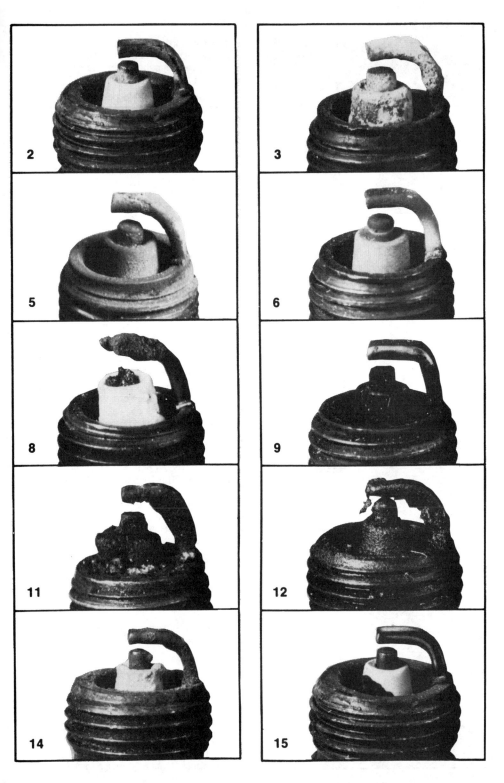

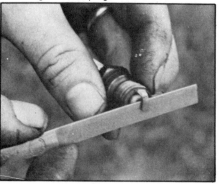

2 File the center electrode so its tip is flat. This is necessary because sandblasting not only removes the deposits, but rounds off the electrodes as well.

3 Whether you are using cleaned plugs or new ones always check the gap. Use a round feeler gauge to do this and set the gap for the specifications for your engine and year of car. Push the wire gauge into the gap and then pull it out. If there is a slight drag or friction between the wire and electrodes' surfaces, the gap is correct. If the gauge goes in easily or falls through, then the side electrode must be bent down toward the center electrode to narrow the gap. Use a special bending tool for this.

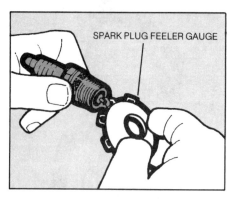

SPARK PLUG FEELER GAUGE

4 Recheck the gap and repeat the bending process until you get the correct gap.

5 If you can't push the gauge into the gap, then the gap is too narrow and the side electrode must be bent up from the center electrode. Don't worry if you don't get it right the first time. Even the best pros have to bend the electrode several times before they get the correct gap.

STOP Some models with electronic ignition (HEI) use special wide gap spark plugs (up to .080 inch). Do not try to open ordinary plugs up to this gap or the electrodes will wear unevenly.

Replace faulty plugs

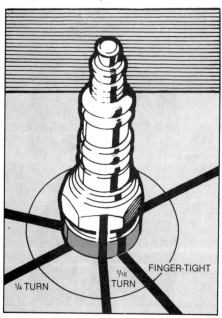

1/16 TURN

FINGER-TIGHT

1/4 TURN

Spark plugs should normally be replaced every 12,000 miles. The recommended replacement interval is longer than that on 1975 and later models that use unleaded gas, but changing plugs at the above mileage will often head off any problems. Replace any plug that has been dropped or has a cracked porcelain. When replacing plugs, make sure you buy the right ones. For proper combustion, you must install plugs that have the correct heat range, the same thread reach, and the same seat design as the ones originally in your engine.

1 Wipe the threads and plug seat in the cylinder head with a clean cloth.

2 Screw the plugs in by hand until they are finger-tight.

3 If you're using tapered seat plugs (no gasket), tighten them 1/16 of a turn with a wrench. Gasket-type plugs should be tightened 1/4 of a turn beyond finger-tight. If you have a torque wrench, tighten the plugs to specs.

How to avoid getting caught in the "crossfire"

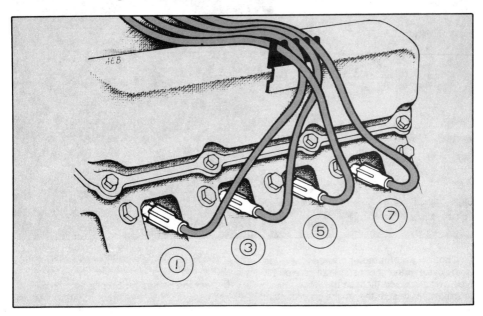

Crossfire is a word used to describe a condition that allows high voltage from one cable to jump or to induce electric current in an adjacent cable, thereby firing its spark plug out of turn. Crossfire is serious because it can damage the inside of a cylinder. The engine will run rough even though the ignition system, carburetion, and spark plugs are OK. If you think your car is suffering from this condition, check the firing order of the engine and find out if two cables serving cylinders that fire consecutively in the same cylinder bank are routed parallel to each other. For example, if cylinder five fires right after cylinder three, make sure the cables are separated in the cable bracket.

Inspect and test spark plug cables

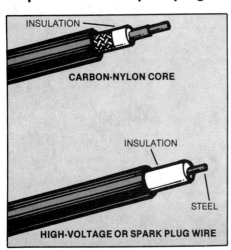

Suppression-type spark-plug cables, known as TVRS (Television-Radio Suppressor) are standard equipment today because they prevent radio and television interference. But you may find that conductor wire (metal core) cables have been installed at some point in your car's life. If your car has this kind of cable, replace it with the suppression-type. Make sure you also replace the wire from the coil to the distributor cap.

1 Inspect the cables for cracks, burns, oil, and grease. Bend them and check for brittleness or deterioration. If a cable fails the inspection, replace the entire set of cables, not just one or two. Defective wires are a common cause of missing and hard starting.

2 To test plug cable resistance, remove one cable at a time from the spark plug and the distributor cap.

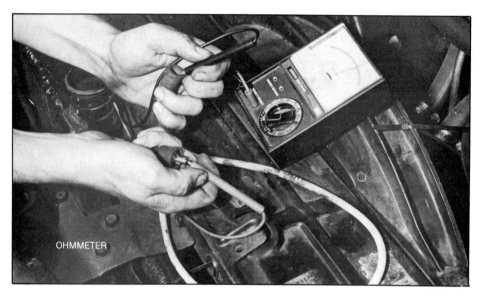

OHMMETER

3 Connect an ohmmeter between the ends of the cable. If the ohmmeter leads are probe type, you can insert them so they touch the terminals. Make sure they make good contact. If your meter has alligator clips, you can make contact with the spark plug end of the cable by inserting a screwdriver into the boot and attaching the alligator clip to the shank of the screwdriver. The other end of the cable will accept an alligator clip.

4 If resistance is more than 30,000 ohms for cables up to 25 inches long and 50,000

ohms for cables longer than 25 inches, as a rule of thumb you should replace the cables.

5 Test the cables for breaks. Sometimes spark plug cables have breaks that are not visible to the naked eye. To test them, attach one end of a jumper wire to a screwdriver blade and the other end to a good ground.

6 Disconnect a cable from its plug. The engine should be running for this test. Using an insulated tool so that you don't get a shock hold the plug cable away from the engine and make sure it doesn't arc (ground).

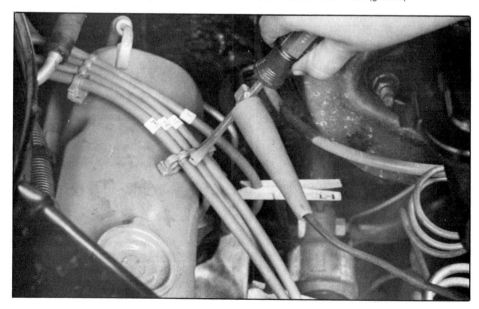

7 Pass the screwdriver blade along the length of the cable. If sparking occurs, it means there's a break in that cable and it should be replaced.

8 Test the other plug cables in the same way.

When the screwdriver blade nears the exposed spark plug end of the cable, it may spark. On 1975 and later models, test each wire as quickly as possible because running with a disconnected plug cable can overheat the catalytic converter.

Install spark plug cables

1 Avoiding cable mix-up is the trick here. Disconnect one cable from the distributor cap tower and from the spark plug and then lay it aside. Take a new cable about the same length as the one just removed (it can be slightly longer) and install it, first in the distributor cap and then to the spark plug.

2 Do this for each of the cables, making sure they are firmly attached.

3 When removing the old cable from the distributor, inspect the cap for corrosion or damage. If you find such a condition, replace the cap, clean it with a small terminal-socket brush or otherwise correct the problem before you hook up the rest of the cables. Also, make sure new cables are correctly routed in the cable bracket to avoid "crossfire." Most suppression-type plug cables have fragile carbon and fiber cores that are easily broken by rough handling, so don't pull, bend or twist them any more than is necessary. Always suspect plug cables if you car is misfiring or is hard to start, especially in damp weather.

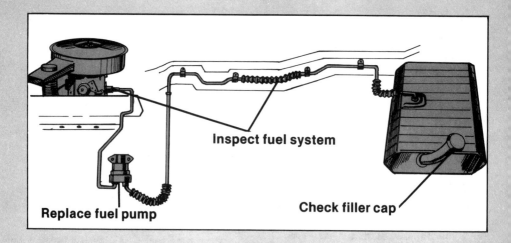

Inspect fuel system

Replace fuel pump

Check filler cap

FUEL

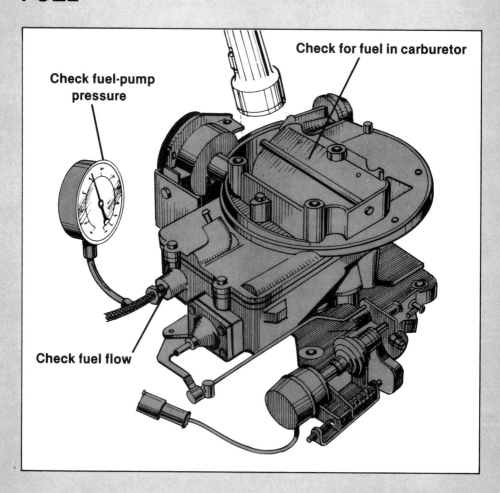

Check for fuel in carburetor

Check fuel-pump pressure

Check fuel flow

9

Fuel System Service

PREP: Make sure there is enough gasoline in the tank to run the engine.

1 **Inspect fuel system.** Carefully check the system for leaks by starting at the carburetor inlet and tracing the fuel line all the way back to the fuel tank. If there are any leaks or damaged lines, repair or replace them as necessary (p. 78).

2 **Check for fuel in carburetor.** Remove the top of the air cleaner, hold the choke plate open, and shine a flashlight into the carburetor while opening and closing the throttle (p. 79). There should be a small stream of gasoline each time the throttle is opened. This confirms that the accelerator pump is working.

3 **Check filler cap.** If the vent in the cap sticks, the engine can starve for fuel (p. 80).

4 **Disconnect ignition.** To prevent the engine from starting during testing, remove the coil wire from the center of the distributor cap and ground it with a jumper wire. With electronic ignition (HEI), disconnect the feed wire (pink) from distributor (p. 80).

5 **Check fuel flow.** This tells you if gasoline is flowing freely from the tank through the fuel pump to the carburetor. Disconnect the fuel line at the carburetor inlet and have a helper crank the engine (p. 80).

6 **Check fuel-pump pressure.** This test tells you if the fuel system is capable of providing enough fuel to the engine for all operating conditions (p. 81).

7 **Replace fuel pump.** If the flow or pressure tests indicate a defective pump, you should replace it (p. 82).

Essential. Basic tools • Flashlight • Cutting pliers • Towels or clean rags • Vacuum/ pressure gauge.

Handy. Remote starter switch • Tubing flaring tool.

Inspect fuel system

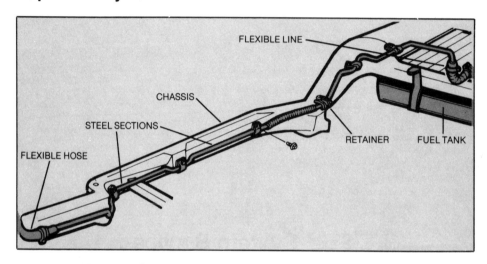

FLEXIBLE LINE

CHASSIS

STEEL SECTIONS

RETAINER   FUEL TANK

FLEXIBLE HOSE

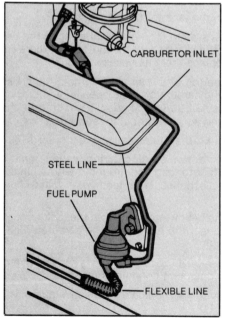

CARBURETOR INLET

STEEL LINE

FUEL PUMP

FLEXIBLE LINE

CAUTION: The fuel system is not complex, but it carries gasoline—a dangerous substance that must be handled carefully.

1 Inspect for fuel leaks by starting at the carburetor inlet. Trace the fuel line to the fuel pump and then back to the fuel tank. If the rubber fuel-line hoses are cracked, damaged, or leaking, replace them.

🛑 Be sure you use only hoses made specifically for fuel lines. Ordinary rubber hose breaks down with gasoline contact, resulting in leaks or a carburetor clogged with rubber particles.

2 Replace the metal parts of the fuel line with new steel line if they are leaking, crushed, or kinked. It's not a good idea to replace just the leaking section of a line, since the unrepaired section may also start to leak after a short time.

3 Complete the basic maintenance procedures described in the chapter on Carburetor Service after you have inspected the fuel system. If you are not having any fuel system problems, your fuel system servicing is finished.

Check for fuel in carburetor

1 Make a quick check to see that there is gasoline in the carburetor if you suspect a problem in your fuel system.

2 Remove the air-cleaner cover and shine a flashlight into the throat of the carburetor. The engine should be off.

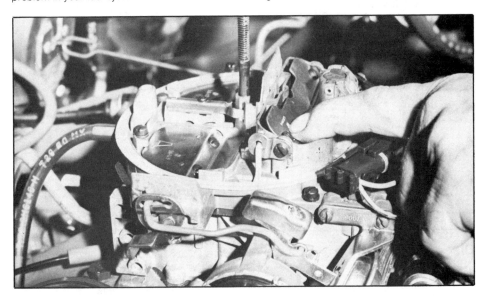

3 Hold the choke plate open. Open and close the throttle or have a helper pump the gas pedal. If you see a squirt of gasoline coming into the carburetor each time the throttle is opened, then fuel is reaching the carburetor. If you are troubleshooting a no-start condition, your problem is elsewhere, and further investigation of the fuel system is not necessary. If gasoline is not coming into the carburetor, proceed to the next step.

Check filler cap

A filler cap is designed to keep gasoline in and dirt out of the fuel tank. 1971 and later models are equipped with a cap that opens to the atmosphere only when the pressure exceeds 3/4 to 1 1/4 psi (pounds per square inch) or vacuum exceeds approximately 1/2 Hg (inches of mercury). If the vent in the cap sticks, the engine can starve for fuel.

Check the pressure/vacuum cap by blowing into the relief-valve housing if fuel is not reaching the carburetor. An instant leak with light blowing—or no release with any amount of blowing—indicates a defective cap. Make sure you replace the cap with one of the same type. In some cases, a defective vacuum vent can keep fuel from reaching the carburetor. If the engine starts and runs with the cap removed, replace the cap. Also, see that the cap's gasket is not damaged.

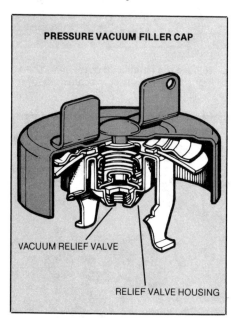

PRESSURE VACUUM FILLER CAP

VACUUM RELIEF VALVE

RELIEF VALVE HOUSING

Disconnect ignition

1 Remove the coil high-tension wire from the distributor center tower to prevent the engine from starting.

2 Ground the coil wire using a jumper wire as described in the chapter on Starting System Service. With electronic ignition (HEI), disconnect the feed wire (pink) from the distributor.

Check fuel flow

This test will tell you if gasoline is flowing freely from the fuel tank through the fuel pump to the carburetor.

1 Disconnect the fuel line at the carburetor inlet and attach a rubber hose to the end of the line.

HOSE

FUEL PUMP

2 Place the hose in a bucket and crank the engine for about ten seconds. A pulsing stream of fuel indicates that the fuel pump is supplying fuel to the carburetor. A trickle of fuel or no fuel at all means the fuel pump is defective, the tank is empty, or the line is blocked between the pump and the fuel tank.

3 To isolate the pump as the defective component, reconnect the ignition system and proceed to the next step.

Check fuel-pump pressure

This test tells you if the fuel pump is capable of providing enough fuel for the engine. The test is performed with a vacuum/pressure gauge connected to the fuel line at the carburetor with the engine idling. To use the gauge, follow the manufacturer's directions.

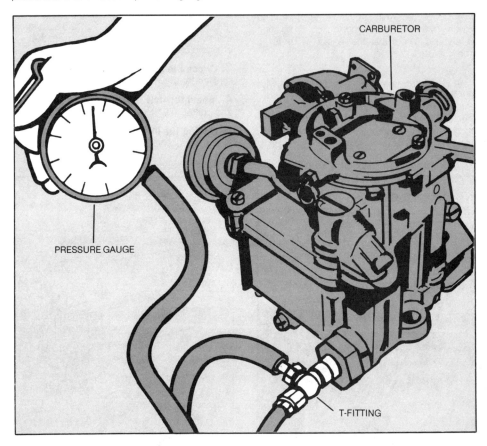

1 **For the typical hookup,** place a T fitting between the carburetor inlet and the fuel line, then connect the gauge to the T. (Some gauge manufacturers recommend that you disconnect the fuel line at the carburetor and hook up the gauge directly to the fuel line. With this method, the carburetor is not connected to the fuel system).

2 **Start the engine** and allow it to idle. It will run long enough on the fuel in the carburetor bowl to complete the test. The pressure should read from 3 to 6½ psi, except as follows: inline 6-cylinder—3 to 5 psi; V-6—4¼ to 5¾ psi; 260 V-8—5½ to 6½ psi; 350 Ventura—3 psi minimum; 265 V-8, 301 V-8, and 400 V-8—7 to 8½ psi; 403 V-8—5½ to 6½ psi; 305 V-8 and Chevrolet-built 350 V-8 with distributor at rear

of engine and clockwise rotor rotation—7½ to 9 psi; Oldsmobile-built 350 V-8 with distributor at rear of engine and counterclockwise rotor rotation—5½ to 6½ psi.

3 **Shut off the engine.** The gauge should remain steady or slowly return to zero. An instant drop in pressure means that the check valve in the pump is bad. Any readings considerably outside of specs indicate a defective pump. However, if the reading is low but you are not experiencing fuel starvation problems, or if it is high but you are not experiencing flooding, the pump can remain in service. Pumps are not repairable, but before replacing yours, make sure the line between the pump and the fuel tank is open. The pump cannot draw gasoline from the tank if the line is blocked, or kinked.

Replace fuel pump

If the tests indicate a defective pump, you should replace it. The job will be easier if you rotate the engine so the low point of the camshaft fuel-pump lobe is against the pump arm. This can be determined by rotating the engine slowing with the pump held loosely in position until you can feel that the tension is removed from the arm.

Note: 1977 and later Astres and Sunbirds with aluminum block 140-cubic-inch four-cylinder engines use an electric fuel pump mounted in the fuel tank. Replacement requires draining and removing the tank. The fire hazard is high and we don't recommend this job for the do-it-yourselfer.

1 Disconnect the fuel lines from the pump and plug the line coming from the tank so fuel will not drain out.

2 Remove the pump attaching bolts and remove the pump and the gasket. Be sure all the old gasket material is removed from the engine block.

3 Check the fuel pump flex hoses and replace them if necessary.

4 Install the new fuel pump, new gasket, and push rod if there is one.

5 Unplug the line from the tank and reconnect the fuel lines to the pump. Start the engine and check for leaks.

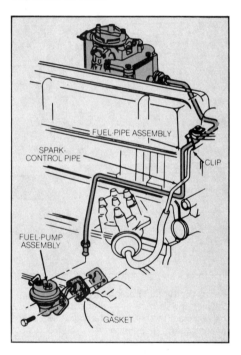

FUEL-PIPE ASSEMBLY

SPARK-CONTROL PIPE

CLIP

FUEL-PUMP ASSEMBLY

GASKET

ECONOTIP The next time you open your trunk, see how much excess weight you are carrying. That 100-pound sack of fertilizer you just never got around to removing can cost you two-tenths of a mile per gallon. If you carry 500 pounds of unnecessary weight, the penalty is one mile per gallon. So if you're not using the excess baggage regularly, clean out the trunk and watch your mileage improve.

PRO SHOP Some V-8 fuel pumps are operated by a short pushrod that tends to fall out of the engine when the pump is removed. To hold the pushrod in place and make installation of the new pump easier, coat the pushrod with heavy grease or petroleum jelly. This will create enough drag to hold the rod up while you bolt on the new pump.

PUMP ARM

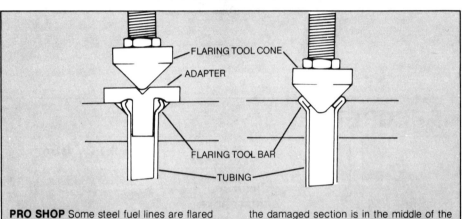

FLARING TOOL CONE

ADAPTER

FLARING TOOL BAR

TUBING

PRO SHOP Some steel fuel lines are flared on the end for better sealing. Replacement fuel line can be purchased from an auto supply store already flared or you can do the flaring yourself with a tubing flaring tool. If the damaged section is in the middle of the fuel line, you can replace the section with a line and two connectors, also available from auto supply stores.

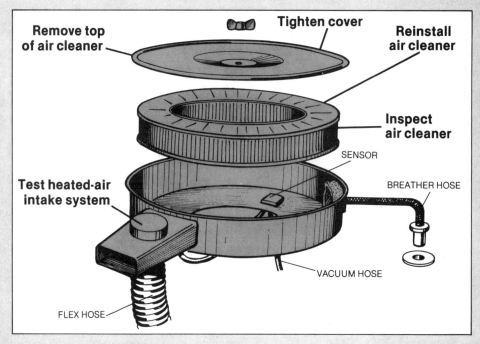

Remove top of air cleaner

Tighten cover

Reinstall air cleaner

Inspect air cleaner

SENSOR

BREATHER HOSE

Test heated-air intake system

VACUUM HOSE

FLEX HOSE

CARBURETOR

Clean EGR valve

Service charcoal canister

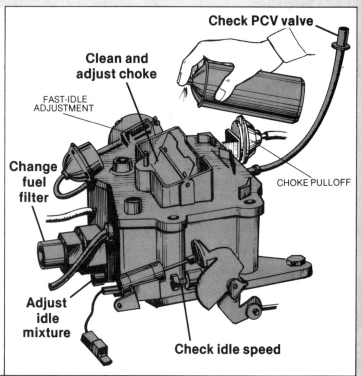

Check PCV valve

Clean and adjust choke

FAST-IDLE ADJUSTMENT

Change fuel filter

CHOKE PULLOFF

Adjust idle mixture

Check idle speed

10

Carburetor Service

1 **Test heated-air intake system.** Make sure the heated-air intake system is working properly. Start the engine; the duct valve should be closed on a cold engine, open on a warm engine. If it is not, check for binding linkage. Inspect the vacuum supply line for cracks, leaks, or restrictions. Check the vacuum motor and the heat-sensing valve (p. 86). Shut off the engine.

2 **Remove top of air cleaner.** It is held on by a wing nut. Inspect the crankcase air filter of the PCV (positive crankcase ventilation) system. Replace if necessary (p. 86).

3 **Remove air cleaner.** Lift out the paper filter element. Disconnect the PCV hose from the side of the air cleaner. Remove the flexible fresh-air duct attached to the snorkel if your car has such a duct. Remove the heat tube from the underside of the snorkel. Tag and remove the vacuum hose(s). Lift the air-cleaner housing off the carburetor and clean it (p. 88).

4 **Change fuel filter.** The fuel filter is located in the carburetor inlet (p. 89).

5 **Clean choke linkages and adjust choke.** The choke should be closed when the engine is cold and open when it is warm (p. 89).

6 **Tighten cover screws and nuts.** They should be snug. Do not overtighten (p. 91).

7 **Clean EGR valve.** Remove the EGR (exhaust gas recirculation) valve from the spacer between the carburetor and the intake manifold and brush off any exhaust deposits (p. 91).

8 **Service charcoal canister.** On 1971 and newer models, make sure the hoses are not hardened, cracked, or plugged. Replace the filter in the bottom of the canister at the manufacturer's recommended intervals (p. 92).

9 **Check PCV valve.** The PCV valve should be replaced according to the manufacturer's recommended intervals or when it becomes clogged. Examine the hose as well (p. 92).

10 **Check and adjust idle speed.** Attach a tachometer to the engine. First set the curb-idle speed, then the fast-idle speed (p. 93).

11 **Adjust idle mixture.** Your car was delivered new with plastic limiter caps installed over the idle-mixture screw(s) to comply with emission control regulations. Satisfactory idle smoothness should be possible within this range. If the cap has been removed, adjust the screw until the best idle is achieved. Recheck curb-idle speed (p. 94).

12 **Remove and reinstall carburetor.** Do this if the carburetor must be overhauled or replaced (p. 95).

13 **Reinstall air cleaner** (p. 95).

Essential. Basic tools • Cutting pliers • Tachometer • Flashlight.
Handy. Hose-clamp pliers • Flare wrench • Wire brush • Fender cover • Pen knife.

Test heated-air intake system

GM engines are equipped with a heated-air intake system to provide warm air to the carburetor during cold running. As air passes over the exhaust manifold, it is warmed and then routed into the air-cleaner snorkel. A valve in the snorkel blends the flow of hot and cold air. Malfunctions in this system are a major cause of hesitation and stalling on acceleration. A stove (air heater) on the exhaust manifold routes hot air from the exhaust manifold to the air cleaner snorkel. To test the system, first make sure the vacuum hoses to the air cleaner and the hot-air duct between the exhaust manifold and the snorkel are intact.

Note: Models with the aluminum block 140-cubic-inch four-cylinder engine do not use this vacuum operated system.

1 Start the engine when cold and let it idle.

2 Shine a flashlight into the snorkel and see if the valve is in the warm-air position—that is, with the air door up so it shuts off air flow through the snorkel. On later models, you'll have to remove a fresh-air duct from the end of the snorkel to view the duct valve.

3 The duct valve will open as the engine warms, so that air is no longer drawn only from the exhaust manifold into the snorkel.

4 If the duct valve isn't working, check to see if it's binding in the air-cleaner housing.

5 Remove the air cleaner and check the vacuum supply lines. Start at the vacuum motor mounted on the snorkel and work back to the source of vacuum. The lines should be free of leaks, cracks, and restrictions.

6 Check the heat-sensing valve (sensor) mounted in the base of the air cleaner if the trouble still isn't found. This valve controls the vacuum motor. There should be vacuum to the valve on the carburetor side. If the engine is warm, there should be little or no vacuum from the heat-sensing valve to the air door vacuum motor. If the engine is cold, there should be vacuum.

7 Turn off the engine.

8 Replace the valve if it is not operating properly.

9 Replace the vacuum motor if there is vacuum to the motor and the heated-air intake valve still doesn't work.

Remove top of air cleaner

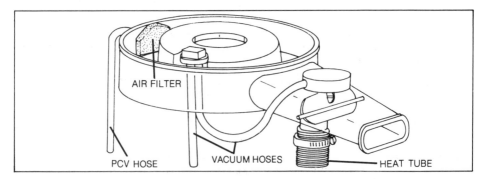

AIR FILTER

PCV HOSE   VACUUM HOSES   HEAT TUBE

The air cleaner is fastened to the top of the carburetor by a wing nut.

Note: Models with the aluminum block 140-cubic-inch four-cylinder engine have a one-piece disposable air cleaner unit.

1 Turn the wing nut counterclockwise until the top of the air cleaner is free.

2 Inspect the PCV (positive crankcase ventilation) air filter mounted on the wall of the air cleaner.

3 Replace the filter if it is clogged or dirty.

4 Inspect the hose and replace it if necessary.

To replace crankcase air filter

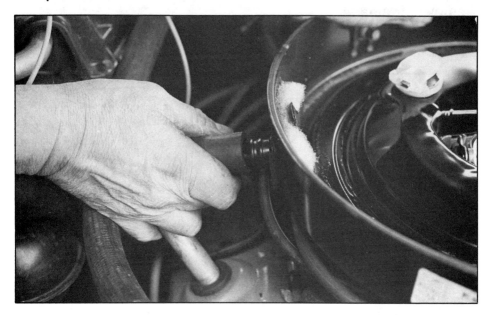

A clip on the outside of the air-cleaner body holds the neck of the PCV fresh-air hose and the filter retainer.

1 To replace the filter element, disconnect the PCV hose by unsnapping the elbow from the retainer clip.

2 Remove the crankcase ventilation filter

retainer clip and the filter retainer from the air cleaner.

3 Remove the filter pack from the retainer, clean out the retainer, and install a new filter.

4 Reinstall the filter retainer, the retainer clip, and the PCV hose, reversing the above steps.

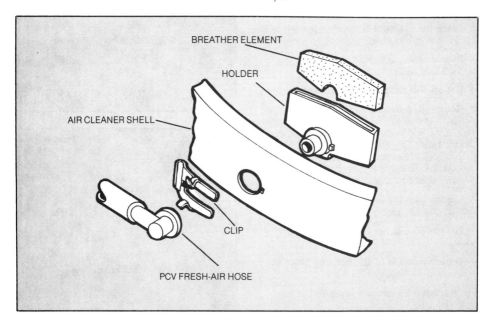

BREATHER ELEMENT

HOLDER

AIR CLEANER SHELL

CLIP

PCV FRESH-AIR HOSE

Remove air cleaner

The filter element keeps dirt out of the carburetor, and it gets clogged over time. If the element is not changed at the manufacturer's recommended intervals, the carburetor will starve for lack of air and waste gas.

1 **Gently lift the air-filter element** from the housing. Be careful not to drop any dust or dirt into the carburetor.

2 **Hold the filter element up to the sky** or examine it with a droplight. If you can see light through the element and there aren't any holes or tears in the pleated paper, it can be reused.

3 **Clean the element** by gently tapping it on a flat surface to dislodge any particles.

4 **Replace the element** if it is clogged, damaged, or wet with oil.

5 **Lift off the body of the air cleaner.**

6 **Remove the fresh-air PCV hose** from the side of the housing, the fresh-air duct from the front of the snorkel if your car has such a duct, and the heat tube from the underside of the snorkel. When removing the housing, lift it up gently to see where the vacuum lines underneath are attached.

7 **Tag the vacuum lines** with masking tape and remove them from their source.

8 **Lift the air-cleaner housing off the carburetor.**

9 **Wipe the inside of the housing clean** to remove any dirt, dust, or oil.

10 **Reattach all vacuum lines** and reinstall the air cleaner.

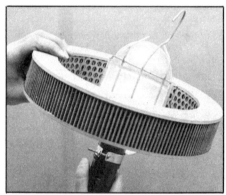

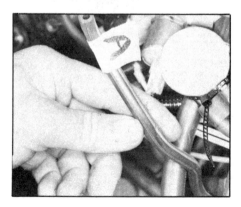

Change fuel filter

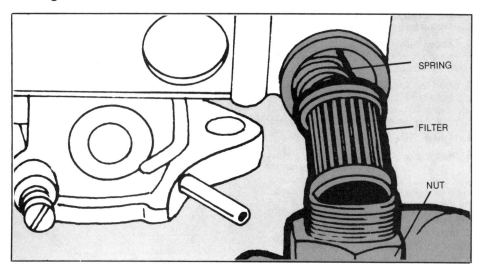

SPRING

FILTER

NUT

If your car hesitates, stalls while cruising, or misses at high speeds, your fuel filter may be clogged. It should be cleaned or replaced. The filter is located in the carburetor inlet. The sintered bronze type may be cleaned, but the pleated paper type must be replaced.

To replace the fuel filter element

1 Remove the air cleaner.

2 Unscrew the fuel line nut from the carburetor inlet fitting.

3 Loosen the fuel line nut at the fuel pump end if necessary to allow the line free movement and to prevent it from kinking or bending when you remove the inlet fitting from the carburetor.

4 Unscrew the inlet fitting from the carburetor and remove the fuel-filter, gasket, and spring.

5 To install a new element, place the spring and the filter in the carburetor inlet.

6 Put the new gasket on the fuel-filter inlet fitting.

7 Screw the inlet fitting into the carburetor and tighten.

8 Install and tighten the fuel line nut in the fuel inlet fitting and tighten the connection at the fuel pump.

9 Start the engine and check for leaks.

10 Reinstall the air cleaner.

Clean choke linkages and adjust choke

The choke limits the amount of air entering the carburetor when the engine is cold. If it doesn't close, the engine may not start; or, if it does, it will hesitate and stall. Chokes are set at the factory and the only maintenance usually required is cleaning. The choke plate is the valve at the top of the carburetor. It is operated by a bimetal spring attached to the side of the carburetor. When the engine is cold, the choke should snap shut when the accelerator pedal is depressed.

To clean choke linkages

1 Visually check the choke plate to make sure it moves freely. If it doesn't, clean the

linkages by spraying carburetor cleaner on all the pivot points. The choke also activates a fast-idle cam which increases the idle speed by holding the throttle open farther than it is when the engine is warm.

2 Spray around the fast-idle cam with the carburetor cleaner while cleaning the choke. The cam should now pivot freely.

3 Check to make sure the vacuum line connected to the carburetor is free of cracks and kinks. The choke has a vacuum assembly that opens the choke plate slightly once the engine is started. This assembly, called a vacuum pullback, is activated by engine vacuum.

To adjust choke

1 Install a tachometer. The engine should be cold. If there are index marks on the choke thermostat cap and the carburetor, make sure they line up properly.

2 Loosen the screws holding the choke cap against the carburetor body just enough so you can rotate the cap with your fingers.

3 Open the accelerator linkage half way and make sure the choke valve is closed. If it is not, rotate the cap until it is. Hold the choke cap in that position and release the accelerator.

4 Tighten the choke cap screws.

5 Start the engine. The choke should open all the way when the engine reaches operating temperature. If the choke doesn't close when the engine is cold and open when it's warm, the thermostatic bimetal spring under the cap may need to be replaced.

6 Note the rpm on the tachometer. The engine will idle fast when the choke is in the On or Closed position. Compare the reading with the EPA decal fast-idle spec. Make sure the adjusting screw is on the correct step of the fast-idle cam.

7 If necessary, adjust the screw that exerts pressure on the fast-idle cam, or follow the instructions on the decal.

8 Snap the accelerator. The engine should drop back to curb-idle speed and the choke should be open.

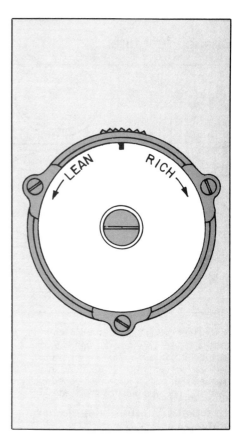

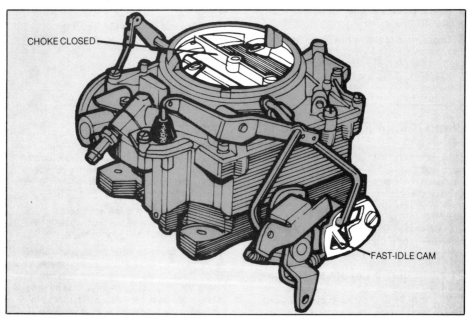

CHOKE CLOSED

FAST-IDLE CAM

Tighten carburetor cover screws and hold-down nuts

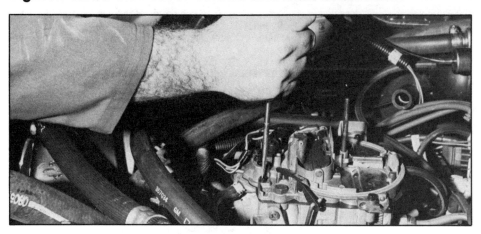

The vibration of a running engine can cause a carburetor's hold-down nuts and cover screws to work loose.

1 Tighten the screws around the top of the carburetor evenly and snugly.

2 Tighten the nuts holding the carburetor to the manifold.

🛑 Be careful not to overtighten the nuts.

Clean EGR valve

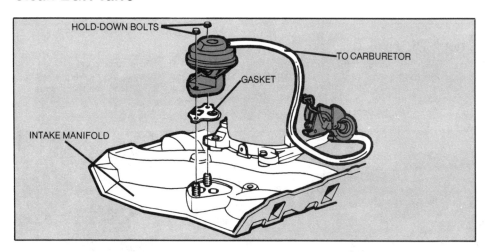

HOLD-DOWN BOLTS

TO CARBURETOR

GASKET

INTAKE MANIFOLD

The EGR (exhaust gas recirculation) valve, which routes exhaust gases back into the intake manifold, is located on the manifold below the carburetor and has a vacuum line running to it. There should be no vacuum at idle. The valve should be cleaned about once a year because exhaust deposit build-up can make the valve stick open and cause rough idling, or clog the valve increasing NOX emission.

1 Remove the EGR valve, the vacuum line, and the screws attached to it.

2 Remove any exhaust deposits that may have built up. Use a wire brush. Do not sand or use solvent.

3 Reinstall the valve. Always install a new gasket whenever the valve is removed for cleaning.

Service the charcoal canister

The charcoal canister is designed to store gasoline vapors that would normally be vented to the atmosphere via the carburetor and gas tank vents. The vapors are stored in the canister and they are drawn into the intake manifold when the engine is running. The canister is located in the engine compartment. All canisters have a filter at the bottom. The filter and/or canister may have to be replaced periodically. Check your owner's manual for the manufacturer's recommended replacement intervals for your car's particular engine and year.

FIBERGLASS FILTER

To replace charcoal canister

1 Tag and disconnect the hoses and loosen the clamps.

2 Lift the canister out and replace it with a new one (usually available only from a dealer).

3 Install the new canister, reconnect the hoses, and tighten the clamps. Make sure the hoses are not hardened, cracked, or plugged.

Check PCV valve

The PCV valve regulates the venting of engine crankcase gases back into the intake manifold so they can be burned. If the valve doesn't function properly, the engine can stall and idle roughly. Also, harmful deposits can form inside the engine. The valve should be changed at regular intervals. Check your owner's manual since the valves differ depending on the engine and model.

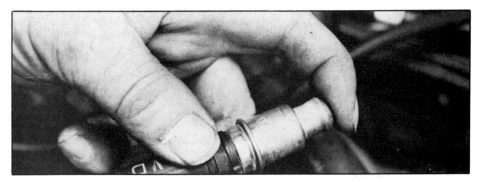

1 Remove the valve and shake it. It should rattle, indicating that the needle in the valve is moving back and forth.

2 Replace the valve if it doesn't rattle.

3 Examine the hose.

4 Make sure there is vacuum at the end of the valve when the engine is running. If not, the valve or its hose is clogged.

To replace PCV valve

The PCV valve is located in the engine rocker cover.

1 Pull the PCV valve out of the grommet in the rocker cover.

2 Remove the valve from the large hose that runs to the base of the carburetor.

3 Install the new valve in the hose, then press its other end into the rocker cover grommet.

Check and adjust idle speed

If your car is equipped with an idle stop or throttle-positioner solenoid on the side of the carburetor, set the idle speed with the solenoid energized (plunger out), by turning the plunger so that it moves in or out against the linkage as required. Then unplug the solenoid wire to allow the plunger to retract into the solenoid. Idle speed should drop. If it doesn't, turn the idle screw on the carburetor linkage out until it does. This will help prevent dieseling.

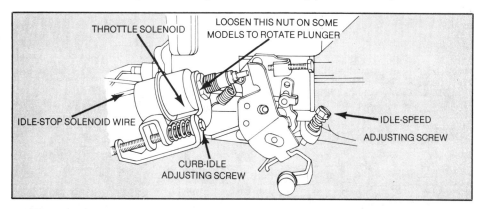

THROTTLE SOLENOID

LOOSEN THIS NUT ON SOME MODELS TO ROTATE PLUNGER

IDLE-STOP SOLENOID WIRE

IDLE-SPEED ADJUSTING SCREW

CURB-IDLE ADJUSTING SCREW

1 Connect a tachometer to the engine.

2 Start the engine and let it idle until it reaches operating temperature.

3 Set the curb-idle speed to the spec on the EPA decal under the hood of your car. When setting curb-idle speed, make sure the choke valve is open. When adjusting curb-idle speed in Drive, have a helper apply the brakes and/or chock the front wheels with bricks and apply the parking brake.

4 Put the transmission in Park (Neutral for manual transmissions) after setting the curb-idle, and set the fast-idle to the EPA decal specs. Open the throttle and rotate the fast-idle cam until the adjusting screw is in the specified position.

5 Turn the fast-idle screw until the specified rpm is reached.

Adjust idle mixture

Engines on all models come equipped with carburetor mixture adjusting screw(s) with a limiter cap(s) attached. The mixture screw should be turned in or out only as far as the limiter cap allows. If the idle becomes rough, adjust the mixture screw until the engine smooths out. You should be able to achieve a satisfactory idle within the range the limiter cap allows. If the cap has been removed, adjust the screw until idle is smoothest. Recheck idle speed.

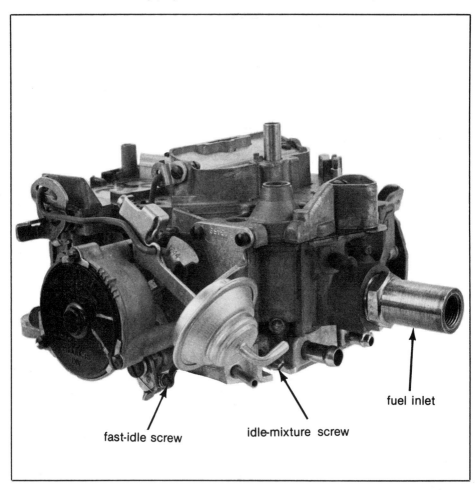

fuel inlet

fast-idle screw   idle-mixture screw

ECONOTIP Do you know when to shut the engine off or when to idle it? Various tests have been carried out by car manufacturers and the federal government to find out whether idling or restarting uses more fuel. Especially with today's frequent gas lines, the right practice may save some fuel. Depending on the study conducted, you should not idle more than half a minute, or a full minute. If the engine idles longer than that, it will take less gas to restart it than to keep it running. It's clear from the studies that anything longer than a minute is wasteful. But your engine may be one of those that should not idle over half a minute. In the long run, you will probably save the most gas by turning the engine off the second you enter the line. That is much better than leaving the engine running in the hope that the line will move quickly and ending up with a total idle time of five minutes.

Remove and reinstall carburetor

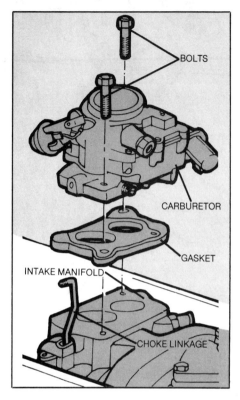

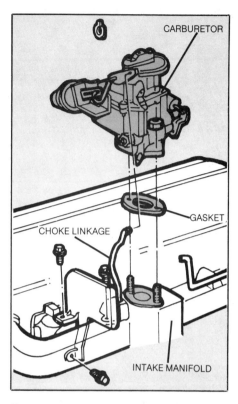

Using this procedure you can remove the carburetor either to disassemble it for cleaning and overhauling or to replace it with a rebuilt or new unit. If you are replacing the carburetor, make sure you buy the correct replacement unit and that you fully understand the terms of any warranty that may be provided with it.

1 Disconnect the battery ground cable to avoid accidental shorts.

2 Remove the air-cleaner assembly from the top of the carburetor.

3 Tag and disconnect all vacuum hoses, wires, and linkages.

4 Disconnect the fuel line at the carburetor.

5 Remove the carburetor attaching bolts and lift off the carburetor and its gasket.

6 Replace the fuel and air filters when replacing the carburetor since they may be contaminated.

7 Install the carburetor and a new gasket on the engine.

8 Replace and tighten the attaching bolts and reconnect all hoses, wires, and linkages.

9 Replace the air cleaner and reconnect the battery ground cable.

10 Start the engine and check for leaks. Correct if necessary.

11 Check the basic carburetor adjustments.

Reinstall air cleaner

If you haven't already reinstalled or replaced the air-cleaner element, do so at this point. Make sure the air-cleaner is flat on top of the car-

buretor and all hoses are attached, then put the top on and tighten the wing nut.

Oil

Remove and replace oil filter

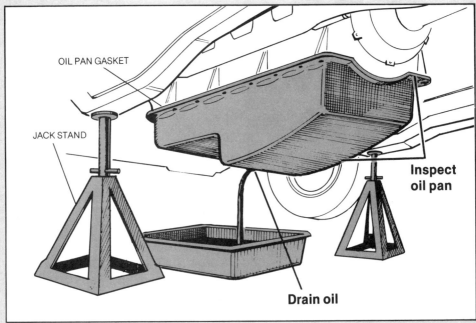

OIL PAN GASKET

JACK STAND

Inspect oil pan

Drain oil

Replace oil

Check valve cover gaskets

11

Oil System Service

PREP: Run the engine for about ten minutes to warm up the oil. Then shut the engine off. Oil flows more easily when it's hot, so this way you stand a better chance of removing most of the dirt and contaminants when you drain the oil. Jack up the front of the car so that you can reach the drain plug. For safety, support the front end on stands and chock the rear wheels.

1 **Drain oil.** Normally, on 1970-74 models, you should change your engine oil at least every four months or every 6000 miles. On 1975-80 models, you should change it every six months or every 7500 miles. Turbocharged engines should get an oil and filter change every 3000 miles. For urban or severe driving, cut this interval in half. After draining the old oil, clean and reinstall the drain plug (p.98).

2 **Inspect oil pan.** Check around the lip of the pan for deterioration or leakage (p. 99). If punctures or holes are found, the oil pan will have to be repaired or replaced. See a professional mechanic.

3 **Check valve cover gaskets.** Inspect the area around the valve cover(s). If the area is damp with oil, then the cover gaskets are leaking and will have to be replaced (p. 99).

4 **Remove and replace filter.** Some pros suggest replacing the oil filter after every second oil change. But if you're going to the expense of putting in clean oil, why contaminate it immediately with the dirty oil left in the old filter (p.101).

5 **Replace oil.** Make sure you're using the correct type, grade, and amount (p.101).

Essential. Basic tools • Jack • Wheel chocks • Safety stands • Drain pan • Rags or paper towels • Oil filter wrench • Engine oil • Oil spout or funnel.
Handy. Fender cover • Flashlight.

Drain oil

1 Warm the engine to operating temperature. Raise and support the front of the car.

2 Place a drain pan with at least a five-quart capacity under the oil-pan drain plug.

3 Loosen the drain plug and remove it and its washer by hand, using the proper size box-end wrench or socket.
CAUTION: The engine oil is hot! After the drain plug is completely unthreaded, pull it and your hand away quickly to avoid burning yourself.

4 Allow the oil to drain completely. It will help if the engine oil filler cap is removed.

5 Clean the drain plug, especially the threads, with a rag or paper towel.

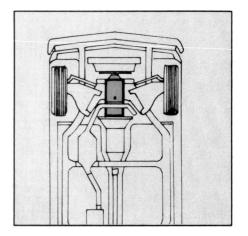

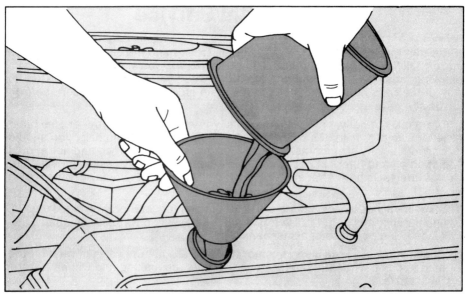

6 Clean the washer. If it isn't badly deformed or cracked, it can be cleaned and reused. If there is any doubt as to its condition, replace it with a new one.

7 Reinstall the washer and plug in the oil pan. Always start the threads by hand to make sure that the plug doesn't cross-thread in the pan.

Inspect oil pan

1 Check around the lip of the pan. If the gasket has deteriorated, there will be leakage and the gasket will have to be replaced.

2 Look for leakage as a result of punctures or holes in the pan.

3 If you find punctures or holes the oil pan will have to be replaced. Do not attempt this procedure yourself but have it done by a professional mechanic.

Repairing the drain plug

Sometimes the threads in the oil-pan drain hole are stripped because the drain plug has been cross-threaded into the hole. If you have this problem, don't worry. You won't have to replace the oil pan. You can repair the drain hole with one of several drain-plug repair kits on the market. One kit uses a self-tapping steel nut, which is forced into the pan's drain hole. A brass plug threads into the steel nut and becomes the new drain plug. Other kits use rubber stoppers.

Check valve cover gaskets

Old or damaged valve cover gaskets can leak, causing oil to seep out over the engine. Inspect the area around the valve cover(s). If you find an oil slick, then the valve cover gaskets should be replaced.

Note: On certain late model V-8 and V6 engines, no valve cover gaskets are used. Instead of gaskets, a silicone sealer is applied to the valve cover to form a gasket. Your local auto parts store will be able to tell you which you need for your car.

To replace valve cover gaskets

1 Remove air cleaner. Tag vacuum lines.

2 Remove and label any vacuum lines, PCV hoses, wires, and spark-plug wires that obstruct the valve cover. If your car has an air pump, it may be necessary to disconnect an air injection hose.

3 On V-8s with air conditioning, loosen the two compressor pivot bolts and the two adjusting bolts. Push the compressor towards the engine and remove the drive belt. Push the compressor away from the engine to expose the valve cover retaining bolts. Remove the rear support bracket.

4 Locate the valve cover retaining bolts.
Inline 6s have eight retaining bolts; V-8s and
V6s have four bolts per valve cover.

5 Remove all retaining bolts and washers.
Note the position of the valve cover to ensure
proper reinstallation.

6 Remove the valve cover. If it sticks to the
engine, tap it lightly with a rubber mallet.

7 Scrape all gasket material from the engine
and valve cover. These surfaces must be clean
if the new gasket is to seal properly.

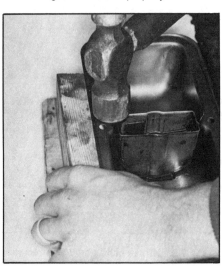

8 Inspect valve cover gasket surface for
high spots around the retaining bolt holes. If
high spots are found, hold the valve cover
upside down, positioning the area with high

spots firmly against a block of wood. Tap the
high spots with a hammer to flatten.

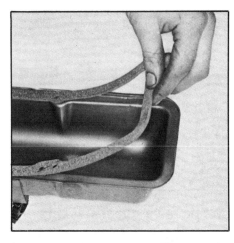

9 Install gasket on valve cover. No gasket
sealer is necessary. To help secure gasket to
valve cover during installation, glue to the
gasket to the valve cover with rubber cement.

Note: Some gaskets have tabs that fit into the
valve cover to hold the gasket in place.

10 Install valve cover on engine.

11 Install bolts and washers and hand
tighten. Tighten bolts carefully with ratchet.
Check bolts several times to be sure they are
tightened equally. If bolts are over-tightened
equally. If bolts are over-tightened, the gasket
will be ruined. (torque specs?).

12 Reinstall the air conditioning support
bracket if it was removed. Reinstall the air conditioning belt and adjust.

13 Reconnect vacuum lines, PVC hoses,
wires, and spark-plug wires.

14 Reconnect air injection hose if it was
disconnected.

15 Reinstall air cleaner.

16 Check engine oil level. Start engine and
check for oil leaks.

PRO SHOP If the gasket falls out of place
during installation, it is likely to leak later on.
To prevent this problem, use the following
sure-fire method. Strip the insulation from five
inches of light gauge wire (16–20 gauge). Cut
away the uninsulated wire. The individual
strands of wire can be used to tie the gasket
to the valve cover through the bolt holes This
procedure may also be used on other gaskets
in the engine.

Remove and replace oil filter

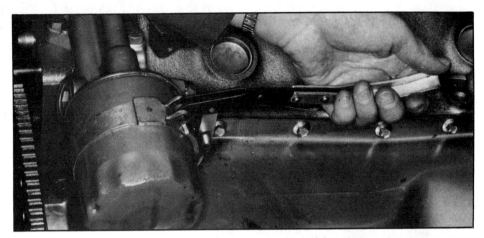

1 Locate the oil filter. It resembles a large can with fluted edges that enable you to grip it with your hands.

2 Set a drain pan under the filter.

3 Use an oil filter strap wrench and loosen the filter by turning it counterclockwise. This may start the oil draining from the filter.

4 Remove the filter by hand when oil has stopped draining into the pan. There will still be some oil in the filter, so remove it in an upright position to prevent spillage.

5 Clean the filter mating surface on the engine with a rag.

6 Coat the gasket of the new filter with a thin film of clean engine oil.

7 Thread the new filter into the engine and make it as tight as you can by hand. Do not use an oil filter wrench. Installation instructions are printed on most filter boxes.

Replace oil

Use only SE or SF grade oil. It is foolish to use bargain oil to save a few cents. The viscosity of the oil is also important. Most oils today are multi-viscosity. That is, they pass the tests for more than one weight. 10W30 or 10W40 is acceptable for most climates and conditions. Single-viscosity oil can be used providing it is the proper weight for the weather.

1 Locate and remove the oil filler cap on the cylinder head (rocker) cover.

2 Use an oil spout or funnel to add the correct amount of oil to the crankcase (usually four quarts plus one for the filter).

3 Check the oil level and add more, if necessary.

4 Start the engine and carefully inspect for leaks around the filter, then turn the engine off.

5 Remove the drain pan and properly dispose of the waste oil and filter in an ecologically satisfactory manner. We suggest you take the oil to a local service station where it will be kept in a tank until sold to a recycler.

COOLING

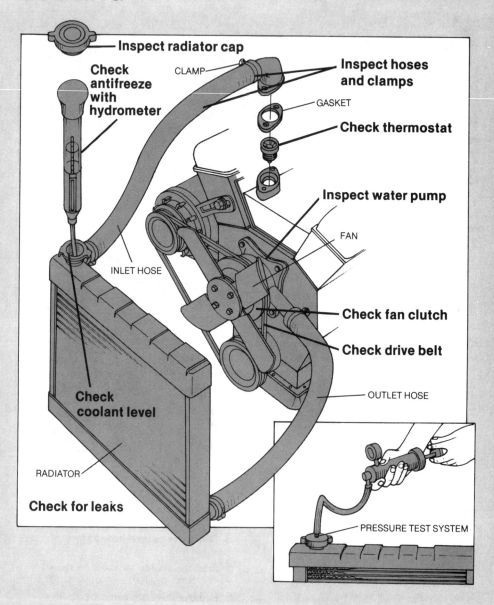

Inspect radiator cap

Check antifreeze with hydrometer

CLAMP

Inspect hoses and clamps

GASKET

Check thermostat

Inspect water pump

FAN

INLET HOSE

Check fan clutch

Check drive belt

OUTLET HOSE

Check coolant level

RADIATOR

Check for leaks

PRESSURE TEST SYSTEM

12

Cooling System Service

1 **Check for leaks.** Inspect the radiator around seams, petcock, automatic transmission oil cooler connections, hose connections, and block and drain plugs. Corrosion or antifreeze stains are a good indication there's a leak (p. 104).

2 **Inspect hoses and clamps.** Check the rubber for cracks, softness, brittleness, leaks, swelling, and chafing. Replace any hoses that show these conditions (p. 107).

3 **Inspect radiator cap.** If it's loose, replace it. Check the pressure relief valve for firm spring action (p. 108).

4 **Check coolant level.** Water should cover the tubes inside the upper tank. Suspect a leak if the level is low. If there are signs of oil, heavy rust, or scales inside the filler neck, you may have an internal leak. Take a compression test. Clean and reverse-flush the system (p. 110).

5 **Check antifreeze with hydrometer.** For best protection, maintain a 50 percent antifreeze, 50 percent water mixture (p. 111).

6 **Inspect water pump.** With the belt removed, grasp the fan pulley with both hands, turning and moving it inward and outward. If it makes a noise when you spin it and/or exhibits excessive side-to-side movement, the bearings are worn. If you see signs of coolant leakage, the seals are probably damaged. Leaks and/or bad bearings mean the pump should be replaced (p. 111).

7 **Check drive belt.** Try to turn the alternator pulley by hand. If it moves, the belt is slipping and should be adjusted (p. 112).

8 **Check thermostat.** Do this only if your engine is overheating or running too cool. Replace a faulty thermostat, and always replace the gasket; never reuse the one you took off (p. 113).

9 **Check fan clutch.** If your car is equipped with a fan clutch and you have an overheating problem that you can't trace to anything else, the fan clutch may be faulty (p. 115).

Essential. Basic tools • Garden hose • Antifreeze hydrometer • Pressure tester and pressure cap adapter • Drain pan • Cloth or paper towels • Putty knife or gasket scraper.

Handy. Compression gauge • Flushing T • Filler neck deflector • Belt tension gauge • Thermometer • Feeler gauges • Wire or string.

Check for leaks

Pressurized cooling system and coloring in the antifreeze make external leaks easy to locate visually. Inspect around the radiator seams, where the core is soldered to the tanks, and around hose connections, petcocks, cylinder head gaskets, block plugs, drain plugs and, if your car is equipped with an automatic transmission, at the connections of the transmission oil cooler lines. If there is an external leak, there could be telltale whitish corrosion or antifreeze stains. Leaks must be corrected mechanically. The radiator must be removed and taken to a specialist. If there are no visible signs of leakage, but your engine has been overheating or you have been replacing coolant frequently, perform a pressure leak test.

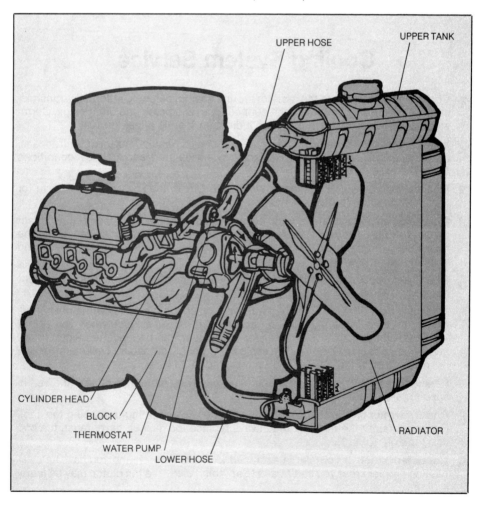

UPPER HOSE UPPER TANK CYLINDER HEAD BLOCK THERMOSTAT WATER PUMP LOWER HOSE RADIATOR

To test for leaks

1 With the engine cool, remove the radiator cap.

2 Start the engine and allow it to heat up to normal operating temperature (at least 150°F). If necessary, add water to the cooling system.

3 Turn the engine off.

4 Install the pressure tester on the radiator filler neck, following the manufacturer's instructions.

5 Operate the pump of the radiator pressure tester until the gauge's needle reaches 15 psi (pounds per square inch).
CAUTION: Never exceed the prescribed pressure. If you do, you may damage the cooling system by rupturing the radiator or splitting the hoses.

6 Look for leaks in the radiator hoses and connections, the heater itself, its hoses and connections, the thermostat housing gasket, the radiator tanks and core, and the water pump.

7 If no leaks are present, the reading should hold for at least two minutes. If no leaks are detected visually but the pressure gauge needle drops quickly, there may be an internal leak caused by a cracked block, cylinder head, water jacket, or, most commonly, a blown head gasket. Go on to the next step.

8 Release the pressure, then reattach the tester and pump to 7 psi. Start the engine and watch the gauge as you rev it a few times. If the needle fluctuates or if pressure builds up

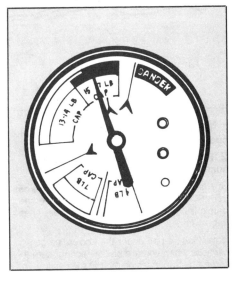

very quickly, compression/combustion pressure is getting into the cooling system, probably through a head gasket leak. Have your car checked by a professional mechanic.
CAUTION: If there is an internal leak, pressure can build up to tremendous levels very quickly. Do not allow pressure to exceed 20 psi.

9 When the pressure test is completed, slowly release the pressure in the cooling system. Refer to the manufacturer's instructions for releasing pressure.

10 Remove the tester from the radiator.

To service the radiator

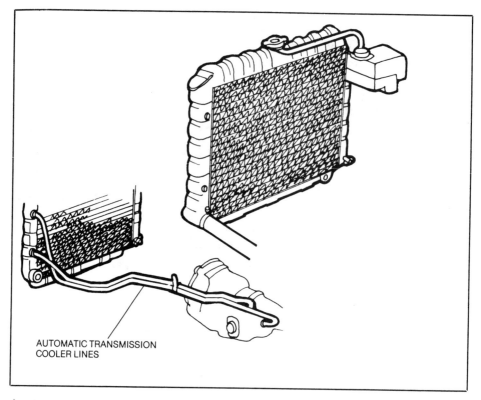

AUTOMATIC TRANSMISSION
COOLER LINES

1 To remove the radiator, first drain the cooling system.

2 Remove the upper and lower radiator hoses.

3 Disconnect the transmission cooler lines from the radiator if your car has an automatic transmission, and plug the ends of these lines to prevent fluid loss.

Note: Place a pan under the cooler line connections when you are disconnecting them to catch any transmission oil that may spill.

🛑 Do not start the engine. If you do, you will lose a great deal of your transmission fluid.

4 If your car has a radiator shroud, remove the bolts that hold it and move it away from the radiator, toward the engine.

5 If your car has a coolant recovery system, disconnect the hose from the overflow tank.

6 Lift the radiator out of the engine compartment.

When lifting the radiator out, be careful not to rub it against any sharp objects, such as

the fan. If you do, you may damage it. And don't cut yourself on the radiator fins.

7 The radiator can now be taken to a local radiator repair shop and you will have saved a good portion of the cost by providing the labor to remove and replace the radiator.

8 To install a repaired or new radiator, reverse the above procedure.

9 Fill the cooling system with coolant, start the engine and allow it to reach normal operating temperature (at least 150°F).

10 Replace the radiator cap and check for leaks.

To check the transmission oil

You may lose transmission fluid when you disconnect the automatic transmission oil cooler lines from the radiator. So when you button up the job, check the transmission fluid to make sure it meets the manufacturer's recommended level, and add ATF (Type A Dexron or Dexron II) if necessary.

Inspect hoses and clamps

Periodically make it a point to inspect all hoses for cracking, rotting, chafing, extreme softness, or extreme weathering. Replace any hose that is in questionable condition. Although some hoses deteriorate faster than others, if one hose is found to be in poor condition, it's a good idea to check the rest of the hoses.

1 Check the hoses when the engine is cold. When you squeeze them, they should feel firm, and when you release them they should return to their shape immediately. Pay particular attention to the bottom hose. Some-

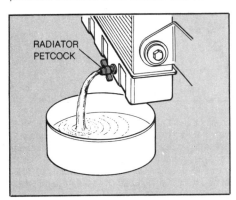

RADIATOR PETCOCK

times there is a spring inside to prevent the hose from being drawn closed. If it gets rough treatment from the water pump, the spring can collapse when the hose softens. If the hose is loose or cracked, air can get into the system, causing rust. Soft hoses are particularly dangerous because they can deteriorate from the inside and small pieces of rubber may break off and clog the radiator and heater core.

2 Examine clamps and clamp areas, and replace broken or weak clamps. Look for white and rust-colored deposits around the clamps. They signify a leak. First try tightening the clamp to correct the leak. If this doesn't work, replace the clamp and/or the hose.

To replace hoses and clamps

1 Drain the radiator into a pan by opening the petcock at the bottom of the radiator. When it is completely drained, close the petcock so you won't forget it later.

2 Loosen the clamps at each end of the hose to be removed. This can be done easily with a screwdriver.

CAUTION: Do not place your free hand beneath the clamp in case the screwdriver slips.

If the clamps are damaged, replace them. If they are of the wire-spring type, always replace them.

3 Twist the hose back and forth to loosen it from the connector. Slide the hose off the connections when free. If the hose is dried and cracked and remnants of it remain on the connectors, clean the connection thoroughly with a scraper or a putty knife, then smooth it with sandpaper. Do not pry under the hose because the connector is soft and may be damaged. If the hose won't budge, split its end with a knife and peel it off.

4 Position the new clamps on the new hose at least 1/8 inch from each end of the hose, and slip the hose on the connector.

5 Tighten the clamps, making sure each one is positioned beyond the bead and in the center of the clamping surface of the connector.

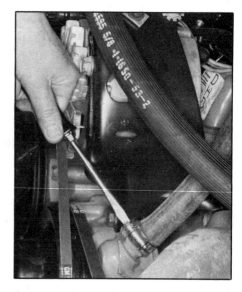

6 Add fresh coolant in the proper amount for your engine.

7 Start the engine and check for leaks.

Inspect radiator cap

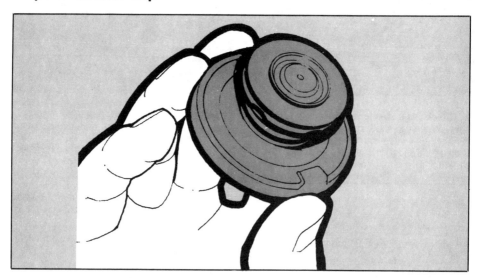

Pressure caps are important to the cooling system. They increase the temperature at which the coolant boils, increase water pump efficiency, and eliminate coolant loss due to evaporation. Defective caps can cause overheating, which could ultimately result in engine damage. A radiator cap should fit tightly on the filler neck.

Replace it if it's loose. Inspect the pressure relief valve. Its spring action should be firm when you press down on it. On cars equipped with coolant recovery systems, the cap allows coolant to flow into the overflow tank when it expands, then allows it to be drawn back into the radiator when it contracts.

To test the cap for pressure

1 Connect a radiator pressure cap adapter, supplied with a pressure tester, to check the relief pressure. Wet the cap's rubber seal with water and connect the cap to the adapter.

2 Read the markings on your pressure cap to determine the rated capacity in pounds per square inch (psi).

3 Pump the pressure tester until the gauge reads slightly less than the rated capacity of the cap. This pressure reading should hold for at least two minutes. If the pressure drops before that time, the radiator cap is defective and should be replaced. A 15-psi cap should vent at 13 to 16 psi.

To clean debris from the radiator

Use a garden hose to clean leaves, insects, and other debris from the radiator. For the best results, apply water at high pressure from the engine side.

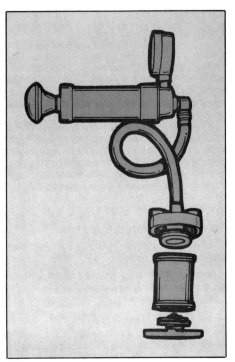

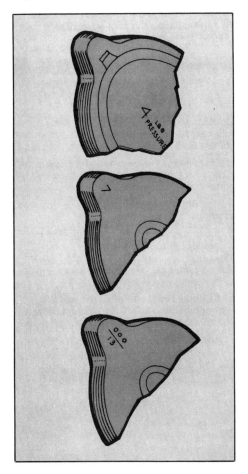

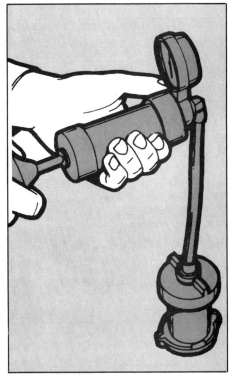

Check coolant level

Coolant should at least cover the tubes inside the upper tank. With coolant recovery systems, the overflow tank should be up to the proper level. If you have been replacing coolant frequently, suspect a leak. If signs of oil, rust, or scales are found inside the upper tank, your car may have an internal leak. While you may not be able to correct this kind of problem, the pressure leak test described above and a compression test can confirm what kind of a leak may exist. If the test proves negative, clean and reverse-flush the system. If, however, the test proves positive, let a professional mechanic check out your engine and cooling system.

To reverse-flush the radiator

1 Drain the cooling system by removing the radiator cap and opening the petcock.

2 Disconnect the upper radiator hose from the thermostat housing and the lower hose from the water pump.

3 Close the petcock and replace the pressure cap.

4 Position the opening of the upper hose so it's pointing toward the ground, away from the engine.

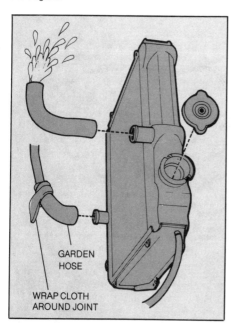

GARDEN
HOSE

WRAP CLOTH
AROUND JOINT

5 Insert a garden hose into the lower radiator hose opening and wrap a piece of cloth around the joint to seal it.

6 Turn on the hose and allow water to flow into the lower section of the radiator, up through the radiator, and out through the upper radiator hose. Keep the water flowing until it is clear.

To use a flushing T

1 Attach a flushing T to the heater supply hose—the hose that goes to the engine. Don't mistake it for the hose that runs directly to the water pump. The T should be situated so that water pouring from it does not get on the alternator.

2 Attach a garden hose to the T and a lead-away hose from the filler neck of the radiator.

3 Put the heater controls on HIGH or HOT, start the engine, turn on the water flow to the garden hose, and watch the water from the lead-away hose until it runs clear. If your radiator has an exceptional amount of grease build-up or corrosion, you may want to use a one-step, fast-flushing agent.

4 After flushing the cooling system, replace the antifreeze.

To reverse-flush the block

1 Remove the thermostat. Now's a good time to check it (see the instructions later on in this chapter).

2 Disconnect the upper radiator hose at the radiator, but leave it connected to the thermostat housing.

3 Disconnect the lower radiator hose at the radiator, but leave it connected to the water pump.

4 Position the hose so the opening faces the ground, away from the engine.

5 Insert a garden hose in the opening of the upper hose. Allow the water to flow through the engine block and out of the water pump through the lower hose to the ground until the water runs clear.

6 Reinstall the thermostat, the housing, and replace the gasket. Connect the upper and lower hoses.

7 Add the proper amount of antifreeze, then fill the radiator with fresh water.

8 Start the engine and allow it to reach normal operating temperature (at least 150°F).

9 Check the coolant level, top off with fresh water, if necessary, reinstall the pressure cap, and check for leaks.
CAUTION: Never flush an overheated engine with cold water, as the thermal shock will crack the block. The same is true when adding water.

Check antifreeze with hydrometer

1 Run the engine and allow the coolant to warm up.

2 Draw off some coolant into a hydrometer-type antifreeze checker.

3 Hold the hydrometer at eye level and read the scale. Some hydrometers use floating balls to indicate the freezing point; others use a floating degree scale. For best antifreeze and anti-corrosion protection, the mixture in the cooling system should be 50 percent antifreeze and 50 percent water.

4 If additional antifreeze is necessary to maintain the desired degree of protection, add enough to reach the 50/50 mixture. To do this you may first have to drain some coolant from the radiator.

Inspect water pump

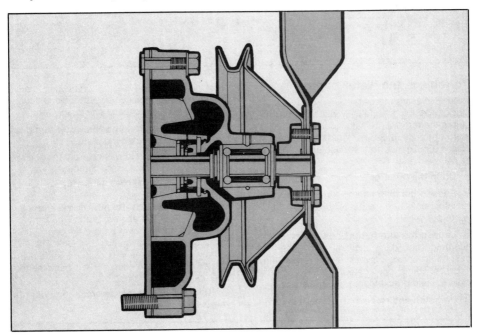

Water pumps are lubricated and sealed at the factory and do not require periodic maintenance. But bearings, seals, and impeller blades do wear out. One cause of bearing failure is excessive tightening of the fan belt.

Note: The water pump on aluminum block four-cylinder 140-cubic-inch engines is driven by the overhead camshaft timing belt.

1 Remove the fan belt and grasp the pulley in both hands. Turn and move it inward and outward. If there is a rough, grinding, or loose feeling, the bearings are probably worn.

2 Check the ventilation hole below and behind the pulley by running your hand over it. If the seal is leaking, your hand will be wet from the coolant. Sand, rust, and other abrasive materials in the coolant will wear away the seal and the impeller blades. Corrosion of the blades and housing may also result from using an antifreeze with inadequate corrosion and rust inhibitors.

3 Replace a water pump that has a leak or worn bearings.

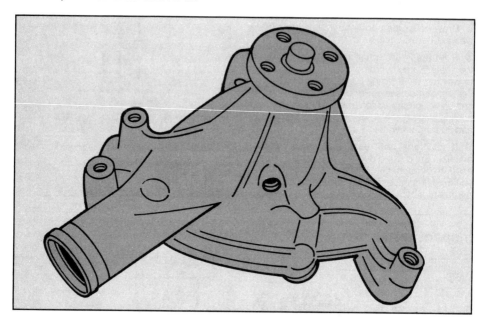

To replace the water pump

Note: Replacing the water pump on aluminum block 140-cubic-inch four-cylinder engines requires the removal, reinstallation, and readjustment of the overhead camshaft timing belt. This is a critical operation best left to a professional mechanic.

1 Drain the radiator.

2 Loosen the clamps and remove the lower radiator hoses and the heater hose from the water pump.

3 Loosen the alternator bolts and pivot the alternator toward the engine. Remove the drive belt. If necesssary on your model, remove any accessory belts (power steering, air conditioning, etc.) and brackets that are in the way.

4 Unfasten and remove the fan pulley.

CAUTION: If the fan is bent or damaged in any way, it must be replaced or else a blade could break off with tremendous and deadly force.

5 Remove bolts holding the water pump to the engine and remove the pump.

6 Scrape off the old gasket from the engine block and clean the surface thoroughly with a cloth. Apply a coating of gasket cement to the new gasket.

7 Lift and position the new pump and gasket against the engine. Start all bolts by hand. Push the pump in toward the engine until it is properly seated against the block. Then tighten the bolts evenly. Be careful not to overtighten or you could snap a bolt. Check the torque specs for your car.

8 Reinstall in reverse order all components removed.

Check drive belt

A loose, worn, or broken alternator belt can cause a serious overheating problem. Inspect the undersides of all belts by twisting them. If they are cracked, cut, frayed, glazed, or covered with grease, you should replace them. Try to turn the alternator pulley by hand. If it moves, the belt is slipping and should be adjusted. More damage can be caused by a belt which is too tight than by one which is too loose.

Check thermostat

Method 1

An easy way to check your thermostat is to remove the radiator cap and insert a thermometer into the radiator. After starting the engine, watch the thermometer. The thermostat has started opening when the coolant begins to flow.

This can be checked by squeezing the upper radiator hose. You will be able to feel the coolant as the engine warms. The thermometer reading should start to rise once the thermostat begins to open.

Method 2

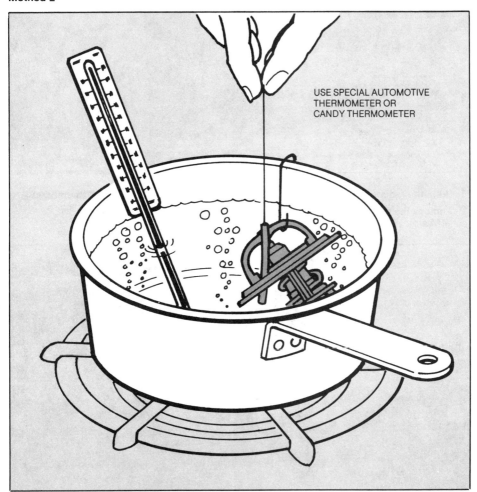

USE SPECIAL AUTOMOTIVE THERMOMETER OR CANDY THERMOMETER

1 Remove the thermostat and put it and a thermometer (which reads up to at least 200°F) into a pan of water.

2 Heat the water and note when the thermostat begins to open. To check the opening temperature, attach a .003-inch feeler gauge to a wire or string and position the gauge between the valve and the housing. When the gauge can be pulled free, you know the thermostat has started to open. Most models are equipped with thermostats that start to open at 190°F or 195°F., and are fully open about 20 degrees higher. If your thermostat doesn't meet specs, replace it.

To replace the thermostat

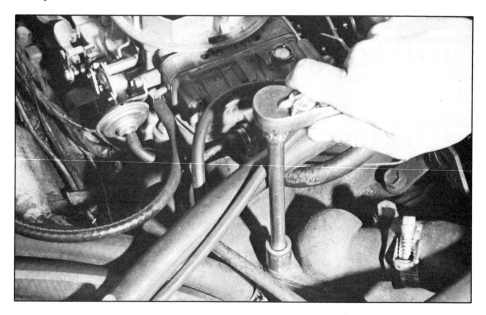

1 Drain the radiator.

2 Remove the radiator hose from the water outlet/thermostat housing.

3 Remove the water outlet/thermostat housing bolts and lift off the housing.

4 Scrape off the old gasket and clean the mating flanges.

5 Install the new thermostat with the spring down.

6 Coat the new gasket with sealer and place it on one flange.

7 Put the water outlet/thermostat housing in place, install the bolts and tighten. Be careful not to snap a bolt.

8 Reconnect the radiator hose and refill the radiator.

Check fan clutch

This device reduces noise and drag on the engine by declutching the fan when it is not needed. If its working fluid is lost or if it is otherwise defective, it can cause overheating. With the engine off and cold, try to spin the fan. You should feel some resistance. If it rotates with no drag (over five revolutions when spun by hand), the clutch is defective and should be replaced.

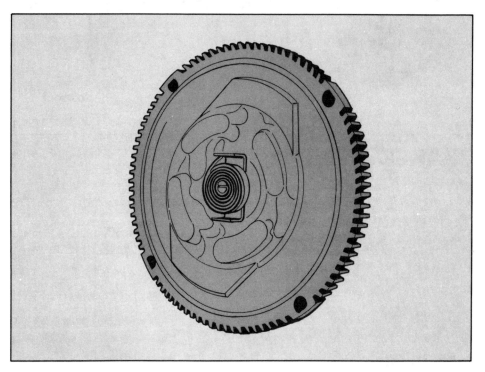

All about fans

The fan and shroud do not require periodic maintenance. However, they should be inspected from time to time. And there's no better time than when you're tuning up your engine. When inspecting the fan, look for bent blades, since these can cause the water pump bearings to wear abnormally. You can do this by physically examining each blade, then, with the engine running, by sighting across the diameter of the fan from the side. Be careful not to let your clothing, hands, or tools get too near the blades. If the blades are bent, the fan will not run "true" and you will see the blades shimmy from side to side. In this case, remove the fan and replace it with one of the same kind. *CAUTION: Do not try to straighten a bent blade or the blade may break and fly off.*

Check the fan shroud to see if it's loose or damaged. A damaged shroud may make noises. Since the shroud works like an air tunnel, your engine may overheat if the shroud is damaged. If it is loose, tighten the bolts. If it is damaged, replace it.

Beware of flying fan blades

There have been numerous cases of fan blades breaking off with terrific force when the engine is running. This could result not only in vehicle damage, but also possible personal injury. Home mechanics working under the hoods of their cars should be extremely cautious about the fan. Fan blades become weakened and a potential hazard for a number of reasons. Examine them carefully and replace the fan if it is fatigued or damaged.

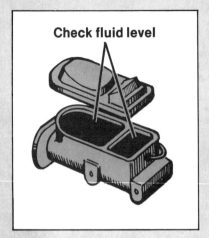

Check fluid level

Inspect
rear brakes

BRAKES

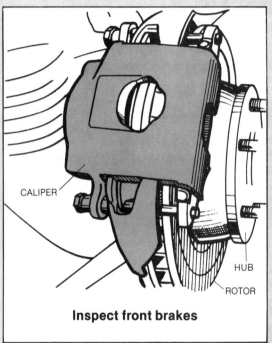

CALIPER

HUB

ROTOR

Inspect front brakes

Check parking brake

Check front
wheel bearings

13

Brake System Service

PREP: Jack up your car and support it on safety stands.

1 **Check fluid level.** Locate the master cylinder under the hood and unlatch its cover. If the fluid level is about 1/4 inch below the top edge of the reservoir, add brake fluid (p.118). If more than 1/4 inch, check the brake system for hydraulic leaks (p.118). Examine the back side of the wheels and tires. If they are wet from hydraulic brake fluid, take your car to a professional mechanic for brake work. Don't attempt to do it yourself. NOTE: With disc brakes, the level in the side of the reservoir that feeds them will fall as the linings wear.

2 **Inspect front brakes.** If your car is equipped with disc brakes in the front, replace the pads (linings) if they are worn to within 1/32 inch of a rivet head or their metal backing at any point (p.119). NOTE: Later models have a wear indicator attached to each pad that contacts the disc and makes a squealing noise when the lining has worn enough to require replacement.

3 **Inspect rear brakes.** You'll have to remove both rear wheel-and-tire assemblies from the axle to do this. If the lining is worn to within 1/32 inch of the rivet heads, replace the shoes (p.126). If the wheel cylinders are leaking, see a professional mechanic.

4 **Check parking brake.** If it fails to hold the car when it is applied, it should be adjusted (p. 130).

5 **Check front wheel bearings.** They should be adjusted if the wheel is too loose or too tight on the spindle (p. 130).

Essential. Basic tools • Allen wrenches • Torque wrench • Flat blade screwdriver • C-clamp (7-inch) • Hammer and chisel or drift • Safety stands • Goggles • Dust mask • Dust solvent • Brake shoe retracting spring tool • Large locking or channel type pliers • Baling wire or coat hanger • Rags.

Handy. Suction bulb • Wire brush • Brake adjusting spoon • Wheel cylinder clamp • Sandpaper • Hold-down spring removing tool • Brake fluid • Brake shoes • Disc brake pads • Brake lubricant • Silicone spray • Grease lubricant (for backing plate).

Check fluid level

If the level of the brake fluid in the master cylinder is too low, the brakes will not work. Warning signs are: Unusually long travel in the brake pedal before the brakes begin to take hold (or the pedal even sinks all the way to the floor); a pedal that feels spongy rather than firm; a pedal that pumps up hard with a couple of strokes. Fluid level should be checked at least twice a year and before long trips. Brake fluid deteriorates chemically over time, so it is a good idea to replace it completely every few years.

1 Park the car on level ground.

2 Locate the master cylinder at the rear of the engine compartment on the driver's side where the brake pedal pushrod comes through the firewall.

3 Wipe around the edge of the cover before you remove it so that no dirt will fall into the fluid. Remove the cover and lay it aside in a place where it will stay clean, but not on a painted surface or within reach of children or pets.

4 Fill the two chambers to within 1/4 inch of the top. Be sure the label on the brake fluid you use says "meets MVSS N. 116, DOT 4 specifications." Don't buy more than a pint of fluid at a time. Keep the cap on tight because brake fluid has a tendency to absorb moisture from the air, which can cause boiling and corrosion in the hydraulic system. Store it as you would poisonous material.

5 Put the top back on the master cylinder. If you allow any dirt to get in, you will have to drain and replace the fluid.

6 Test the brakes (if the car is equipped with power brakes, do this with the engine running and the transmission in Neutral or Park). If the pedal feels firm and normal, test the brakes with the car in motion.

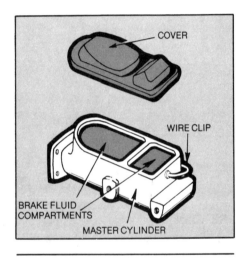

COVER

WIRE CLIP

BRAKE FLUID COMPARTMENTS

MASTER CYLINDER

Checking for fluid leaks

If the brake fluid level in the master cylinder reservoir is low, check for leaks at the wheel cylinders, calipers, hoses, lines, connections, and master cylinder cap. Since disc brake calipers take more and more fluid as the pads wear, if the side of the reservoir that feeds the front brakes isn't topped off occasionally, the level will be low even if there is no leak.

If your car has power brakes and loses fluid, but you can't find the leak, perhaps fluid is getting past the master cylinder's seal into the power brake booster where it is drawn by vacuum. If this is the case, you'll probably find fluid in the hose that runs from the engine intake manifold to the booster.

Leaks at a wheel cylinder or caliper are usually revealed by fluid that spreads to the inside of the wheel and tire.

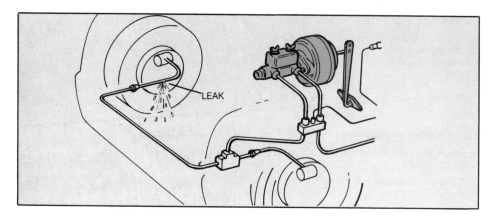

Flexible brake hoses that go to the front calipers or cylinders and between the chassis and the rear axle are often overlooked. If one cracks or ruptures, braking power in that half of the system will be completely lost, so inspect them carefully. Unless you are an advanced do-it-yourselfer who thoroughly understands the fine points of brake hydraulics (how the dual master cylinder works, proper bleeding procedures, etc.) you should entrust any repairs on this system to a competent mechanic.

CAUTION: Brake linings are made of asbestos, and care should be taken when working on your car's brakes. Wear a mask to avoid inhaling brake dust. A special spray solution, available at auto supply stores, will keep brake dust from flying into your face when you clean the backing plate and other brake parts.

Inspect front brakes

If you have noticed that your brake pedal must be pushed harder or closer to the floor than usual, or if you have been hearing a scraping, screeching noise coming from the front when you apply the brakes, the chances are the shoes or pads are worn and the rivets are scraping against the brake discs or drums. Continued use will only lead to a more expensive brake job, perhaps requiring replacement of the brake discs or drums. If, after checking the master cylinder and hydraulic system, you find no leaks, this could mean the pads or linings are worn out. Drums should be taken to an automotive machinist to be turned on a brake lathe when you replace the shoes.

1 If your car is equipped with front disc brakes, remove the wheel and tire to expose the disc (also known as the rotor).

2 If either pad (lining) is worn to within 1/32 inch of a rivet head or its metal backing plate at any point, replace both pads. You should replace the pads on the other side of the car at the same time.

3 A first-class job demands that the rotors be removed and taken to an automotive machinist to be trued up on a brake lathe.

4 When replacing linings, disassemble one side at a time so you can refer to the other side for proper reinstallation of parts.

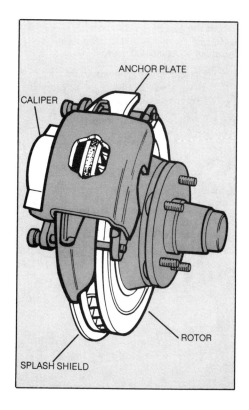

To replace front disc brake pads

Before starting this job, you will probably have to siphon some brake fluid out of the master cylinder. Otherwise when you force the caliper pistons back into their bores, the reservoir will overflow. The following instructions are for replacement of front disc brake pads for 1970-80 models.

For all models except Astre and Sunbird

1 Raise the front of the car and support it safely on stands.

2 Remove the wheel and tire assembly to expose the brakes.

3 Remove the lid of the master cylinder and siphon out and discard two-thirds of the fluid from the reservoir that supplies the front brakes.

4 Position a seven-inch C-clamp on the caliper so that the screw side pushes against the outboard pad and the rigid side is against the back of the caliper cylinder housing.

5 Tighten the clamp until the caliper moves outward all the way so that the piston is forced to the back of its bore. Remove the clamp.

6 Remove the two mounting bolts that hold the caliper to the support bracket.

7 Lift the caliper off the rotor.
CAUTION: Do not allow it to hang by the rubber hydraulic hose. Instead, hang it from a suspen-

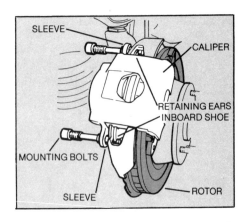

sion part with a bent coat hanger or a piece of wire. Inspect the hose for cracks or other damage and replace it if you find any.

8 Remove the inboard pad, then dislodge the outboard pad.

9 Remove the shoe support spring from the piston, then remove the two sleeves from the inboard ears of the caliper and the four rubber bushings from the grooves in each of the caliper ears.

Note: Do not remove the sleeves and the four rubber bushings from the caliper, as described in step 9, unless new ones have been included with the replacement disc pads. If these parts are not included, the old ones should be left on.

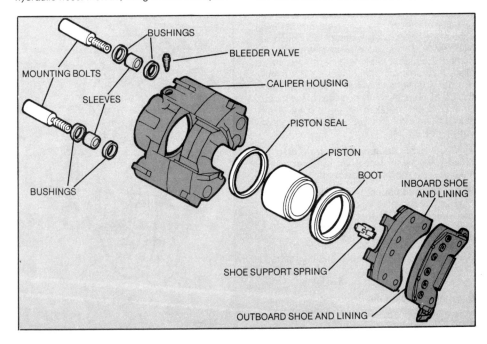

10 If you have removed sleeves and bushings, thoroughly clean the holes and the bushing grooves in the caliper ears, and the mounting bolts.

11 Examine the inside of the caliper for fluid leaks. If you find any, the hydraulic seals should be replaced by a professional mechanic. If there are no leaks, wipe out the inside of the caliper with a cloth. Do not use compressed air as it may dislodge the piston's rubber dust boot.

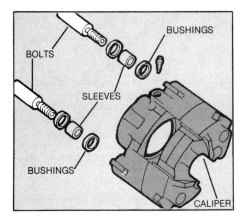

12 For a first-class job, both rotors (discs) should be removed from the car and taken to an automotive machinist to be trued up on a lathe. However, if your car did not exhibit any braking problems, such as pedal pulsation, and if the rotors don't have any obvious damage, you may leave the rotors in place and clean them with #80 grit sandpaper and alcohol.

13 Lubricate the new sleeves, rubber bushings, bushing grooves, and the ends of the mounting bolts with Delco-Moraine silicone grease or its equivalent.

14 Install the new rubber bushings in all four caliper ears.

15 Install the new sleeves in the two inboard caliper ears so that the end toward the pad is flush with the machined surface of the ear. The sleeves can usually be pushed in with your thumb. If they are stubborn, use slip-joint pliers.

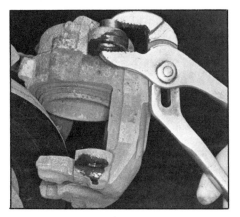

16 Snap the shoe support spring on the back of the new inboard pad so that the end of the spring with the single tang engages the notch in the pad, then place the assembly on the piston with the spring against the inside wall of the piston cavity.

Note: On wear-indicator pads, there are specific left- and right-hand parts. The wear indicator should be toward the rear of the caliper.

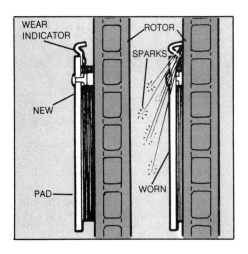

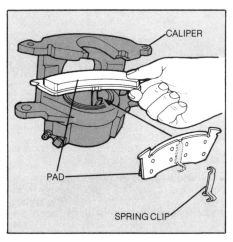

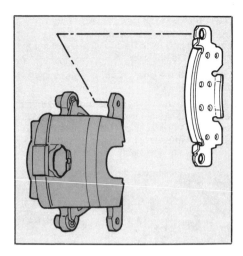

17 Install the outboard pad in the caliper so that its two upper tabs go over the caliper ears and its lower tab engages the caliper cut-out. Again, note left- and right-hand pads.

18 Position the caliper back over the rotor, being sure the brake hose isn't twisted. Then

line up the holes in the caliper ears with those in the support bracket.

19 Insert the mounting bolts through the sleeves in the inboard caliper ears and under the inboard pad's retaining ears, then into the outboard caliper ears. Torque them to 35 foot-pounds.

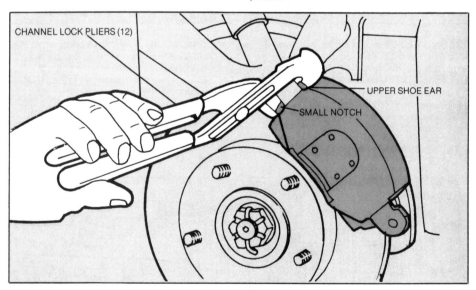

20 Add fresh brake fluid to the master cylinder reservoir and pump the brake pedal to seat the linings against the rotor.

21 Using large locking or channel type pliers, clinch the outboard pad's upper ears by placing one jaw on the top of the upper ear and the other jaw in the notch on the bottom of the

pad. Squeeze until there is no clearance between the ears and the caliper housing.

22 Replace the brake on the other side of the car in the same manner.

23 Refill the master cylinder reservoir with fresh fluid, pump the pedal until it is firm, then recheck the fluid level and install the reservoir lid.

For Astre and Sunbird

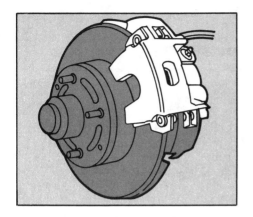

1 Raise the front of the car and support it safely on stands.

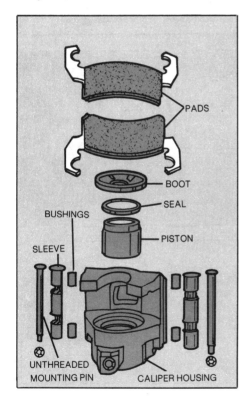

2 Remove the wheel and tire assembly to expose the brakes.

3 Remove the lid of the master cylinder and siphon out and discard two-thirds of the fluid from the reservoir that supplies the front brakes.

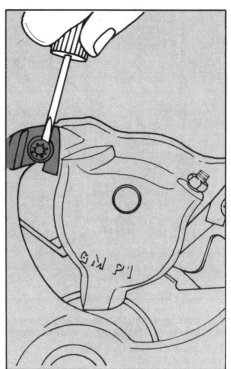

4 Pry the stamped nuts off the inboard end of each mounting pin.

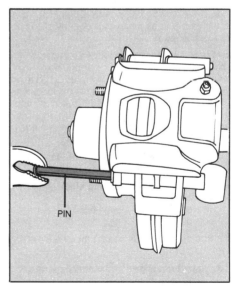

5 Pull out both mounting pins, using pliers. Lift the caliper off the anchor plate. Do not twist or stretch the hydraulic hose.

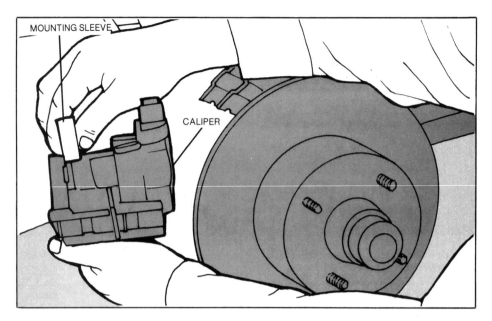

MOUNTING SLEEVE

CALIPER

6 Remove the inboard and outboard pads by sliding them to the mounting sleeve opening.

7 Remove the mounting sleeves and bushing assemblies.

8 Examine the inside of the caliper for fluid leaks. If you find any, the hydraulic seals should be replaced by a professional mechanic. If there are no leaks, wipe out the inside of the caliper with a cloth. Do not use compressed air as it may dislodge the piston's rubber dust boot.

9 For a first-class job, both rotors (discs) should be removed from the car and taken to an automotive machinist to be trued up on a lathe. However, if your car did not exhibit any braking problems, such as pedal pulsation, and the rotors don't have any obvious damage, you may leave the rotors in place and clean them with #80 grit sandpaper and alcohol.

10 Clean the caliper sliding surfaces with a wire brush to remove rust and dirt.

11 Install the new mounting sleeves and bushings in the caliper grooves. The shouldered end of the sleeve must be toward the outside.

12 Install both pads so that their ears are over the sleeves.

13 Place the caliper on the anchor plate and slide in the mounting pins.

14 Press the stamped nuts on the mounting pins using a socket that is the right size to contact only the outer edge of the nut.

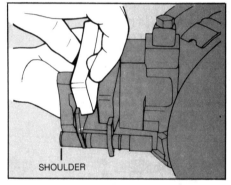

SHOULDER

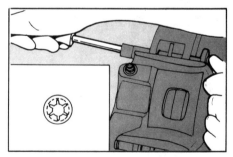

15 Do the brake on the other side of the car in the same manner.

16 Refill the master cylinder reservoir with fresh fluid, pump the pedal until it is firm, then recheck the fluid level and install the reservoir lid.

To replace front drum brake shoes

1 Raise the car and support it on stands.

2 Remove the wheel-and-tire assembly. Do one side at a time to avoid mixing up the parts.

3 Remove the grease cap from the hub and take out the cotter pin. Then remove the nut lock, adjusting nut, and flat washer from the spindle.

4 Grasp the drum and pull it out slightly, then push it back into place. Now you can easily remove the outer wheel-bearing assembly.

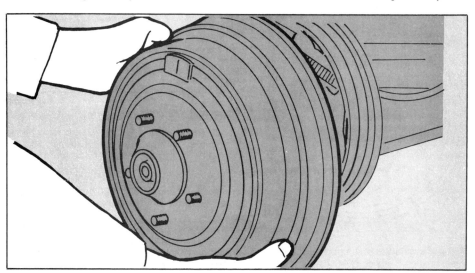

5 Pull the hub-and-drum assembly off the spindle. You may have trouble removing the brake drums. If so, insert an adjuster tool or a screwdriver into the slot in the outside wall of the drum and back off the adjustment. The slot may never have been punched out. If not, look for the outline of the slot cut into the drum and knock out the center with a hammer and drift or chisel. You'll need a small wire hook to pull the self-adjuster blade out of the way while backing off the adjustment. Have the drum

machined, and replace the grease seal.

6 Remove the shoe-to-anchor springs and the self-adjuster return spring and link from the anchor pin. Remove the shoe-guide plate.

7 Remove the shoe hold-down springs, brake shoes, adjusting screw and nut, and the automatic adjuster parts.

🛑 The actuator lever, pivot and override spring are an assembly, so remove them together.

8 Clean the brake plate with solvent and apply brake lube to the pads on the backing plate where the brake shoes contact them. Also, be sure the adjuster screw is free, and apply lube to the threads and socket end.

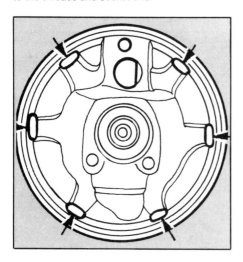

9 Reassemble the brake parts using the wheel on the other side of the car as a reference for proper reinstallation. You can check the automatic adjuster by lifting the lever past a tooth on the adjuster screw. Release the lever and it should push the tooth down. If it doesn't, examine the assembly for proper installation.

10 Fit the drum over the brake lining using the brake drum as an adjusting tool. If the drum goes on easily, remove the drum and expand the brake adjuster. Again, fit the drum over the lining. If it still goes on easily, expand the adjuster a little more.

11 Repeat this procedure until the brake lining prevents the drum from fitting over the brake shoes. When this happens, contract the adjuster a little by rotating it in the opposite direction. Instead of adjusting with the brake tool, use your thumb and index finger.

12 Final adjustment can be made after assembly is completed (and after the car is lowered) by making a few reverse stops. This action allows the self-adjuster to expand the shoes automatically until all excessive clearance between the shoes and drums is eliminated.

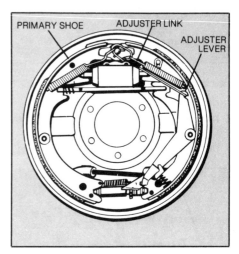

PRIMARY SHOE   ADJUSTER LINK   ADJUSTER LEVER

Inspect rear brakes

If the parking brake fails to hold the car when it is applied, or if the rear wheels are noisy during braking, the brake shoes may be worn out. To confirm this, you will have to remove both rear wheel-and-tire assemblies from the axle. You may have trouble removing the brake drums. If so, insert an adjuster tool or a screwdriver into the slot in the outer wall of the drum. The slot may never have been punched out. If not, look for the outline of the slot cut into the drum and knock out the center with a hammer and drift or chisel. To back off the adjustment, you'll need a small wire hook to pull the self-adjuster blade out of the way. If the drums still won't come off, hit them between the wheel studs with a hammer to break them free from the axles. If the shoes are worn to within 1/32 inch of the rivet heads, they should be replaced. Further operation of the brakes in this condition will lead to serious scoring of the drums and they may have to be replaced.

Note: The 1975 Astre has a more complex brake arrangement than other models. We recommend you leave brake inspection to a pro.

Photo Steps: Rear brake replacement

Raise the car and support it on stands. Remove the wheel-and-tire assembly from the drum. Don't disassemble the brake on the other side of the car at this time. When you reassemble the brake parts on one side, you can use the other side as a reference for installation of parts.

Note: The 1975 Astre has a more complex brake mechanism than other models. We recommend you leave rear brake shoe replacement to a pro.

1 Remove brake drum. If the drum has not been removed previously, you will first have to remove the retaining washers, before sliding the drum off. The retaining washers may be discarded.

2 Note the arrangement of the whole assembly. This is what you will see after the drum is removed.

3 Remove the brake shoe return springs, using a brake spring tool.

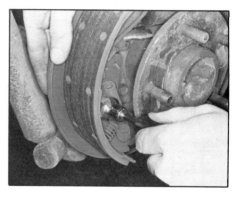

4 Remove the brake shoe hold-down springs using brake spring tool or pliers.

5 Remove the brake shoe guide. Remove all of the parts for the self-adjusting mechanism.

6 Remove the parking brake strut and spring.

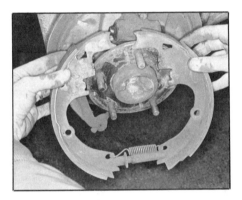

7 Remove the brake shoes from the braking plate with the star adjuster and spring and parking brake lever.

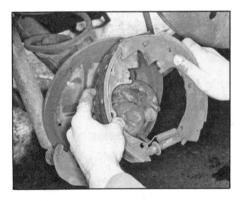

8 Unhook parking brake lever from secondary brake shoe. Crisscross the two brake shoes at the top to free the star adjuster and spring.

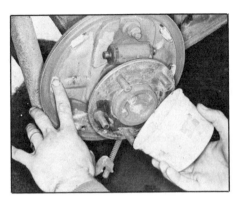

9 Clean backing plate with a wire brush to remove dust. Inspect wheel cylinder and surrounding area for signs of brake fluid leakage. If leakage is suspected see a professional mechanic. Coat the high spots on the backing plate with white grease.

10 Lubricate the star adjuster with white grease. Assemble the adjuster.

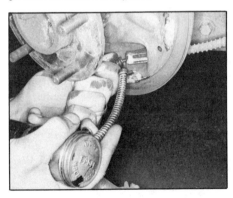

11 Pull back the parking brake cable spring and lubricate with oil.

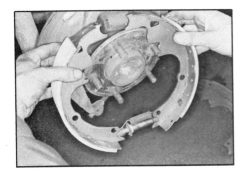

12 **Install the star adjuster spring** to the bottom of both brake shoes. Crisscross the shoes at the top. Install the star adjuster at the bottom between both brake shoes, and even brake shoes out. Be sure star adjuster spring does not interfere with the star adjuster's movement. Hook the parking brake lever to the secondary brake shoe, and install both brake shoes to the backing plate.

13 **Install hold-down spring pins** through the braking plate and brake shoes. Install hold-down spring on primary brake shoe. Install self-adjusting mechanism, then hold-down spring on secondary brake shoe. Use brake spring tool or pliers to install hold-down springs.

14 **Slide the parking brake strut bar**

between the brake shoes. Install shoe guide. Center brake shoes on backing plate, being sure the brake shoes meet the wheel cylinder properly.

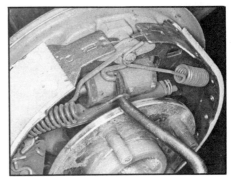

15 **Install self-adjusting actuating link** between the self-adjusting mechanism and pin. Install brake shoe return springs using a brake spring tool.

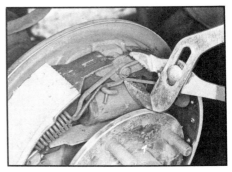

16 **Tighten return springs** around pin using pliers.

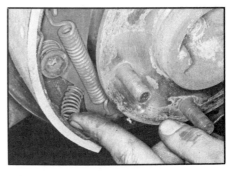

17 **Install spring** between secondary brake shoe and self-adjusting mechanism. Install brake drum and adjust the brakes.

Check parking brake

If the parking brake fails to hold the car when it is applied, and the rear drum brakes are in good condition and have the correct clearance, you should adjust the parking brake.

1 Make sure the parking brake is fully released and the transmission is in Neutral.

2 Block the front wheels and raise the rear of the car. Support it with safety stands.

3 Under the car, tighten the adjusting nut on the single front cable (where it goes through the cable yoke) to cause the rear wheels to drag. Then loosen the adjusting nut until the rear wheel brakes are fully released. There should be no drag.

4 Lower the car and check the operation of the parking brake. If the adjustment does not correct the condition, go back to the discussion on "Inspect rear brakes" and check the rear brake shoes for excessive wear, if you haven't already done this.

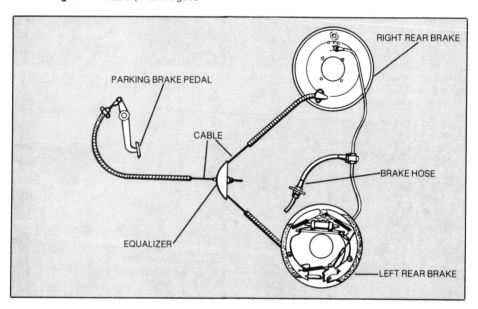

PARKING BRAKE PEDAL

CABLE

EQUALIZER

RIGHT REAR BRAKE

BRAKE HOSE

LEFT REAR BRAKE

Check front wheel bearings

1 Block the rear wheels and raise the front of the car until the tires clear the floor. Support the car with safety stands. Make sure the brakes are not dragging before attempting to spin the wheel. If your car has disc brakes, push the brake pads into the caliper to free the rotor. If it has drum brakes, you may have to back off the adjustment, which will require the removal and reinstallation of the wheel-and-tire assembly.

2 Grasp the tire with one hand at the top and the other hand at the bottom, and rock it in and out several times. You should feel a very small amount of clearance in the bearings but it must not be excessive.

3 Spin the wheel and note if the bearings drag or feel rough.

To adjust front wheel bearings

1 Raise the car and support it safely on stands.

2 Remove the wheel cover or hub cap, then the hub dust cap.

3 Remove the cotter pin and the spindle nut lock.

4 Turn the wheel assembly in the direction of rotation and slowly tighten the adjusting nut until the wheel does not spin freely.

5 Turn the adjusting nut an additional 1/4 to 1/2 turn to seat the bearings. If you have a torque wrench, tighten the adjusting nut to 17–25 foot-pounds while rotating the wheel to seat the bearings.

6 Back off the adjusting nut about half a turn or until the wheel begins to spin freely. Now, tighten the nut as much as you can with your fingers, or, if you have an inch-pound torque wrench, tighten to 10–15 inch-pounds. To verify the adjustment, grab the wheel at the top and bottom and rock it back and forth. Feel for any excessive looseness in the bearings. Remember, wheel bearings should never be preloaded—they need some clearance or they'll run hot and wear out prematurely.

7 Place the nut lock on the adjusting nut so one of the cotter pin holes in the spindle will align with one of the castellations of the nut lock. If the holes don't line up, back the adjustment off until they do. Install a new cotter pin.

8 Check the wheel rotation to be sure it rotates freely and install the grease cap and hub cap. If rotation is noisy or rough, disassemble the hub and inspect the bearings.

9 Lower the car and, if equipped with disc brakes, pump the brake pedal several times before driving the car to establish lining-to-rotor clearance and to restore normal pedal travel. Readjust drum brakes by backing up and stopping several times.

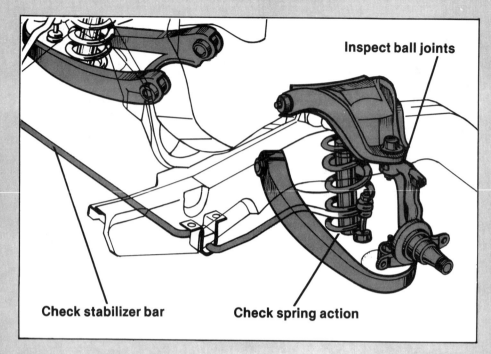

Inspect ball joints

Check stabilizer bar

Check spring action

SUSPENSION AND STEERING

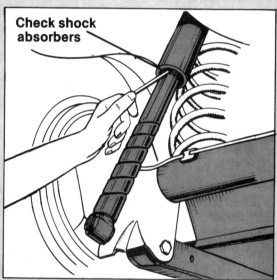

Check shock absorbers

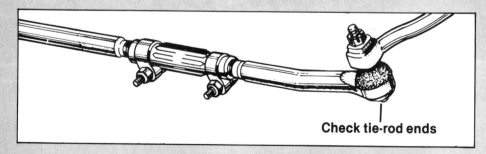

Check tie-rod ends

14

Suspension and Steering Service

PREP: Inflate tires, including the spare, with the correct air pressure. The tire decal on the door pillar or the glove compartment door gives you the recommended air pressure for cold inflation and the load limits for the manufacturer's recommended tire size. Each tire has its size and maximum cold inflation pressure molded into the outer sidewall. Make sure the gas tank is full and the spare tire is in the place designed for it. Unload everything else from the trunk and passenger compartment. Remove any heavy dirt, clay, mud, ice, or snow from the chassis and underbody. Set the front seat(s) in rearmost position.

1 **Check spring action.** You don't need any tools to do this, just your eyes. If you must have your car's front end aligned, sagging or broken springs will prevent the mechanic from doing a good job (p. 134).

2 **Inspect ball joints.** Worn ball joints cause poor tire wear and faulty wheel alignment. Inspect upper and lower ball joints (p.134) and, if they're worn, have a professional mechanic replace them (unless you're an advanced do-it-yourselfer).

3 **Check shock absorbers.** Inspect both front and rear shocks. Good shocks are important for safe driving. Replace them when they're worn or leaky (p. 137).

4 **Check tie-rod ends.** Faulty tie-rod ends can result in front-end wander and should be replaced (p. 141).

5 **Check stabilizer bar.** If you hear a thumping sound when you drive, suspect sway-bar bushings. If they have deteriorated or are missing, they must be replaced (p. 142).

Essential. Basic tools · Jack · Jack stands.

Check spring action

As your car ages, its springs lose their supporting height (they sag) and sometimes even break. So to make an accurate inspection of the front and rear suspension, you must check each spring. When it comes time to have your car's front end aligned because of poor tire wear or handling problems, sagging or broken springs will prevent the mechanic from doing a proper job because ride height directly affects the front-end geometry.

1 Observe your car's position on level ground. If you notice any abnormalities at any of the four corners of the car, investigate the low corner(s) for a broken or sagging spring.

2 If the coils of a front spring are touching or very close together, the spring is worn or broken. Rear leaf springs, which are normally slightly convex while supporting a car, will either be level or concave when they are worn or broken.

3 Go to a professional mechanic to correct any spring problems.

Note: When having springs replaced, do it in pairs.

Inspect ball joints

Worn ball joints are a potential cause of poor tire wear and faulty wheel alignment. Even more important, they are dangerous. If a ball joint breaks, the spindle that holds the front wheel may become detached from the car. Aligning the front end with defective ball joints is false economy. If you need ball joints, have them replaced before you have your car aligned.

3 Have a helper grasp the tire and rock the wheel in and out while you observe the upper end of the spindle and the upper suspension arm. If you see or feel any movement at all between the upper end of the spindle and the

To inspect the upper ball joint

1 Raise the car and place safety stands under the lower suspension arms as close as possible to the lower ball joint without blocking it from view.

2 Make sure the front wheel bearings are adjusted and the ball joints lubricated.

upper suspension arm, the upper ball joint is worn.

4 Have the ball joint replaced by a professional mechanic.

To inspect the lower ball joint

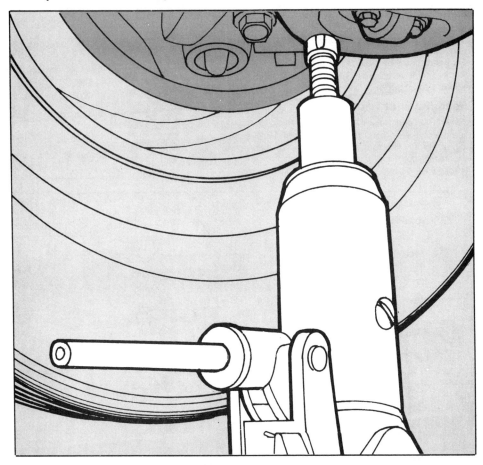

1 Raise the car and support it with a safety stand under the lower suspension arm close to the ball joint.

2 Insert a pry bar or pipe between the tire and the ground.

3 Have a helper pry up on the bar as you observe the ball joint and suspension arm.

PRO SHOP: To remove troublesome ball joints; jack up your car and support it by the body, not the frame. Remove the cotter pin and back off the attaching nut three-quarters of the way. Using a 5-pound hammer, give both sides of the steering knuckle a few shots, jarring the ball joint out of the steering knuckle. Put a jack stand under the lower control arm and release the weight off the suspension components.

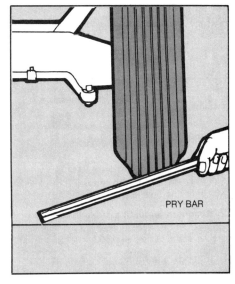

PRY BAR

4 The amount of allowable vertical play in the ball joint ranges from .020 to .060 inch, depending on the year and model. If you see more than 1/16 inch of vertical play, you probably need a new ball joint, but have the car checked by a professional mechanic with a dial indicator to be sure.

Wear-indicator ball joints

Many 1973 and newer models have wear indicators in their lower, load-bearing joints. This helpful feature allows you to tell for certain whether or not a ball joint has worn out. Check as follows:

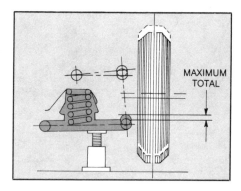

MAXIMUM TOTAL

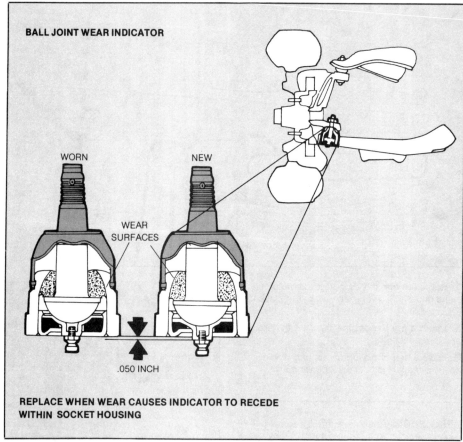

BALL JOINT WEAR INDICATOR

WORN

NEW

WEAR SURFACES

.050 INCH

REPLACE WHEN WEAR CAUSES INDICATOR TO RECEDE WITHIN SOCKET HOUSING

1 Leave the car on the ground with its weight on the tires.

2 Reach underneath each lower suspension arm and clean off the area where the grease fitting projects down from the ball joint.

3 If the grease fitting is screwed into a shoulder that projects from the bottom cover of

the ball joint, then your car is equipped with indicators.

4 When new, the shoulder (indicator) projects .050 inch from the ball joint's bottom cover. As wear occurs, the shoulder recedes. If you find that the shoulder is flush with the cover or countersunk into it, it is definitely time for the ball joint to be replaced.

Check shock absorbers

Good shock absorbers are important for safe driving. Their job is to keep the tires in contact with the road by limiting suspension undulations. When shocks are worn, the wheels hop on the road, which can cause loss of steering control or braking power, cupped tire wear, and/or poor riding quality.

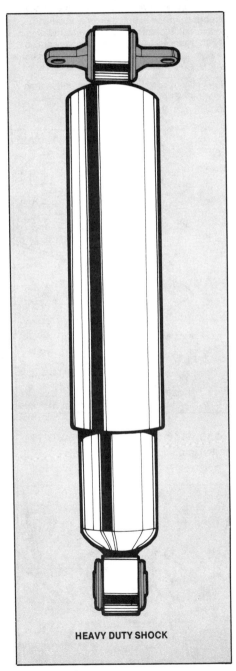

HEAVY DUTY SHOCK

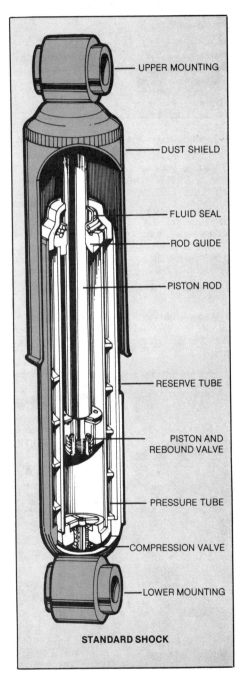

UPPER MOUNTING

DUST SHIELD

FLUID SEAL

ROD GUIDE

PISTON ROD

RESERVE TUBE

PISTON AND REBOUND VALVE

PRESSURE TUBE

COMPRESSION VALVE

LOWER MOUNTING

STANDARD SHOCK

6 Inspect all shocks for leaks. A light film of fluid is OK. Make sure any suspected leak is actually coming from the shock and not from another component. Leaking shock absorbers must be replaced.

7 Disconnect the lower end of the shock absorber, grasp it, and then pull down and push up as fast as possible. Use as much shock travel as you can. The action should be smooth and uniform through each stroke. If it is not, replace the shock.

Note: Higher resistance in one direction than in the other is normal. So are swishing noises coming from the shock.

1 Push down on one of the car's fenders or bumpers as far as you can.

2 Release your hold and immediately push down again. Do this several times until the car begins to bounce.

3 Stop pushing when the car is at its lowest point and allow it to bounce back. The car should settle after moving to the bottom and returning part way up. If the car continues to bounce, the shocks are worn and must be replaced.

4 Jack up the car and support it on safety stands to check further.

5 Inspect the shocks visually to make sure they are securely and properly installed and the shock insulators (bushings) are not damaged or worn.

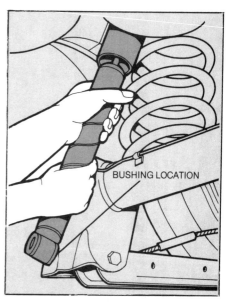

BUSHING LOCATION

To replace front shock absorbers

1 Raise the car and support it safely on stands.

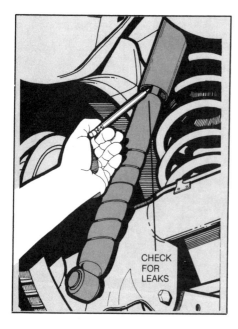

CHECK FOR LEAKS

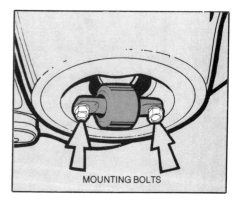

MOUNTING BOLTS

2 Hold the flat at the top of the piston rod with a wrench or a pair of locking pliers while you loosen the upper piston rod nut with an end wrench. Remove the nut, washers, and bushing.

3 Remove the lower mount bolts.

4 Lower the shock absorber out through the hole in the lower suspension arm.

5 Extend the new shock absorber, put the washer and bushing on the piston rod and raise the shock absorber into place.

6 Install the lower mounting bolts.

7 Place the bushing, washer, and top nut on the piston rod and tighten the nut until the bushing begins to swell at the sides. Do not crush the bushing.

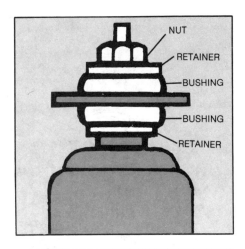

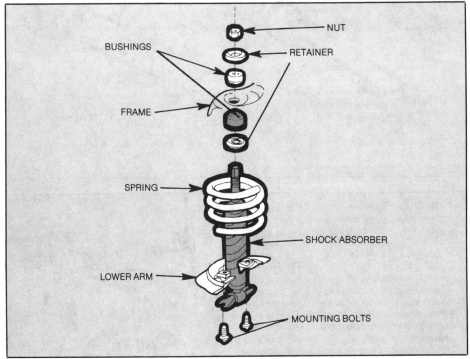

To replace rear shock absorbers

Check the rear shocks the same way you checked the front ones.

1 Raise the rear of the car and support it safely on stands.

CAUTION: If your car has rear coil springs, be certain to support the rear axle with stands or a jack on the side you are working on. If you don't, the axle will fall dangerously when the shock absorber is removed.

2 Remove the upper mounting nut. Note the placement of the washers.

3 Unscrew the lower mounting nut and remove the shock absorber.

4 Put the new shock absorber in place and install the nuts. Be sure the washers are in the right order. Tighten the nuts.

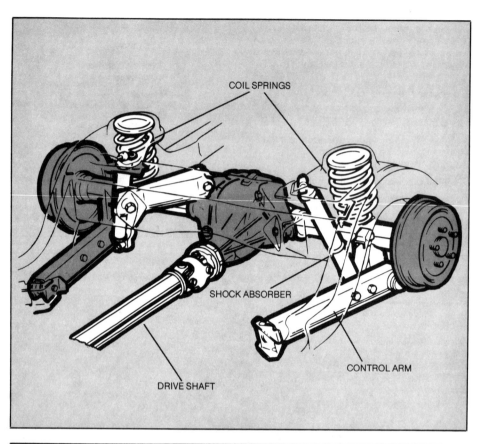

COIL SPRINGS

SHOCK ABSORBER

DRIVE SHAFT

CONTROL ARM

PRO SHOP Shock absorbers can be extremely hard to remove due to frozen nuts and bolts, so apply plenty of penetrating oil to them and allow it sufficient time to work (a whole day isn't too long). If they still won't budge, you may have to resort to extra leverage in the form of a pipe slipped over your wrench. Beyond that, the use of a nut cracker or hacksaw may be necessary. Professional mechanics often use a cutting torch to remove frozen shock absorber connectors. If you think yours are going to be a big problem, consider buying the new shocks where installation is included in, or a low cost addition to, the bill.

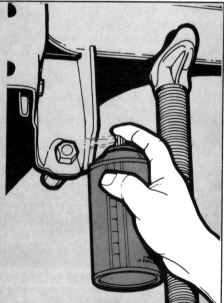

Check tie-rod ends

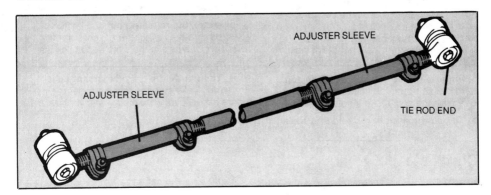

ADJUSTER SLEEVE

ADJUSTER SLEEVE

TIE ROD END

If you've been experiencing front-end wander, your car may have faulty tie-rod ends. A car is said to wander when it drifts either to the right or to the left as the car is driven with the steering wheel held firmly in a straight-ahead position. Do not confuse this condition with a definite pull to one side. Try to locate the play in the steering system by using what's known as the "dry park check." Have a helper rock the steering wheel back and forth (weight on the wheels) while you observe the linkage parts and connections. If you see any lash that looks excessive, that is probably the trouble. Investigate further with the tie-rod end check.

Note: As the steering box wears, lash between its gears increases, and this can cause wander. Excess clearance can be eliminated by adjusting the over-center screw in the top of the steering box. Loosening the locknut and turning the screw in reduces lash. But since over-tightening the screw can cause a dangerous binding condition, we recommend that you have it done by a professional mechanic. If you do it yourself, back the screw out at least half a turn after taking up the clearance, and make sure you have the wheels in the straight-ahead position. Finally, check for binding through the whole range before driving the car.

1 Raise the car and place safety stands under the lower control arm. Chock the rear wheels.

2 Grasp one tire-and-wheel assembly with one hand at the three o'clock position and the other hand at the nine o'clock position. Move the wheel alternately in and out.

Note: For a valid test, restrict the wheel's movement only to its free play. Don't turn the wheel-and-tire assembly so that it moves the steering wheel. If there is movement, suspect the tie-rod end on that side.

3 To verify, have a helper move the tire-and-wheel assembly as you just did, while you observe the tie-rod end socket for excessive play between it and the spindle steering arm.

4 Repeat this procedure on the other front wheel.

To replace tie-rod ends

1 Remove the tie-rod outer end cotter pin and nut with the car in the same position as in step 1 above.

2 Loosen the outer tie-rod adjustment collar clamp.

3 Count the number of exposed threads on the tie-rod/ball socket up to the adjustment collar, or paint them. Make a note of this number to ensure correct reinstallation.

4 Separate the tie-rod end stud from the spindle arm. Use a heavy hammer to strike the side of the spindle steering arm while exerting downward pressure on the tie-rod end. Be certain to support the spindle arm or you could crack it. It will probably take more than one blow to separate the end from the spindle. A puller or separator will make this job easier.

5 Remove the tie-rod end from the adjustment collar. Count the number of turns it takes to remove the end. Make a note of this number.

6 Thread the new tie-rod end into the ad- justment collar the same number of turns it took to remove it.

7 Insert the tie-rod end stud into the spindle.

8 Install the retaining nut and tighten it. Make sure the new cotter pin goes through the nut and the hole in the stud. Bend back the cotter pin ends.

9 Tighten the tie-rod adjustment collar clamp. Make sure the same number of threads are exposed as you noted in step 3 above.

Check stabilizer bar

The stabilizer bar (or sway bar) is attached to the frame by clamps and bushings. It is attached to the lower control arms by links (bolts) and bushings. If the bushings are in good condition, then the sway bar improves handling. But if the bushings have deteriorated, you will hear a thumping sound when you drive.

1 Jack up the car and place safety stands under the lower control arms. Chock the rear wheels.

2 Inspect the bushings visually. They may be crushed or even missing. If so, they must be replaced. Replacement bushings come as a set, so replace them all at the same time.

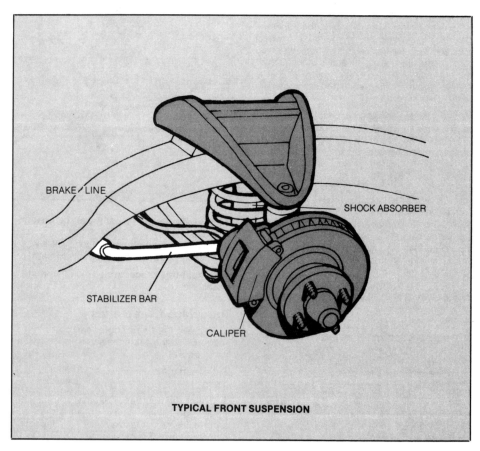

BRAKE LINE

SHOCK ABSORBER

STABILIZER BAR

CALIPER

TYPICAL FRONT SUSPENSION

To replace front stabilizer links and bushings

1 **Jack up the front** of the car and support it with stands. It is OK to place jack stands under the lower control arms, but do not block stabilizer link bolts. Remove the wheel.

2 **Remove the stabilizer link bolt,** washers, bushings, and spacer.

Note: Remove and install one stabilizer link at a time. You can thus compare the one you have replaced to the old one, to be sure it is assembled correctly.

3 **Install a washer** and a bushing on the new link bolt. Insert the link bolt part way into the lower control arm. (In the following steps it will be necessary to push the bolt in further as each part is added.)

4 **In between** the control arm and the stabilizer shaft, install the following items in the order given: bushing, washer, spacer, washer, bushing.

5 **With the link bolt** protruding through the stabilizer shaft, install a bushing, washer, and a nut.

6 **Tighten the link bolt** until bushings are slightly compressed. Replace wheel.

To replace front stabilizer bar bushings

1 **Jack up the front** of the car and support it with stands.

2 **Remove** both stabilizer bar brackets.

3 **Remove and discard** the old bushings.

4 **Install new bushings** on the stabilizer shaft. Install the new bushing with the slit facing forward.

Note: If the new bushings are difficult to install, spray with silicone grease to ease installation.

5 **Install stabilizer bar brackets** and tighten bolts. If torque wrench is available, tighten bolts to 24 foot-pounds. To ease installation of stabilizer bar brackets, it may be necessary to support the stabilizer bar with a jack or other support.

PRO SHOP To keep stabilizer bushings and all other rubber bushings in good condition, spray with silicone grease at each oil change.

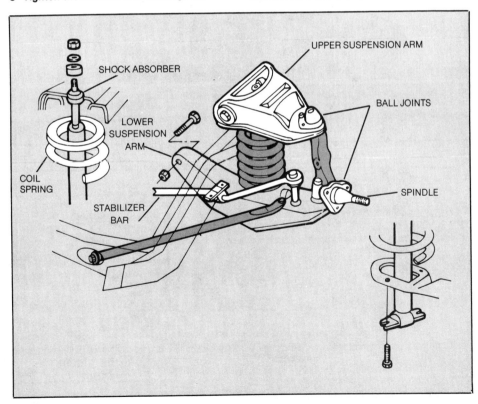

SHOCK ABSORBER

UPPER SUSPENSION ARM

BALL JOINTS

LOWER SUSPENSION ARM

COIL SPRING

STABILIZER BAR

SPINDLE

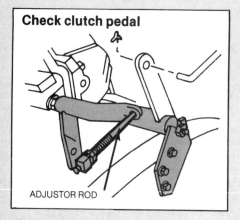

Check clutch pedal

ADJUSTOR ROD

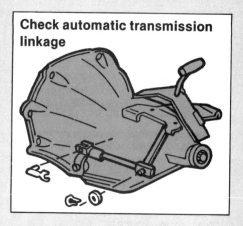

Check automatic transmission linkage

CLUTCH AND TRANSMISSION

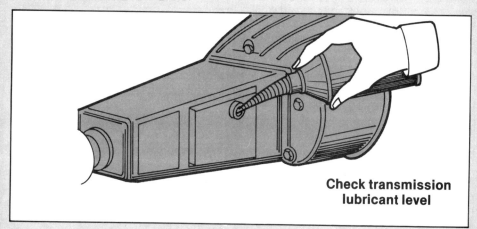

Check transmission lubricant level

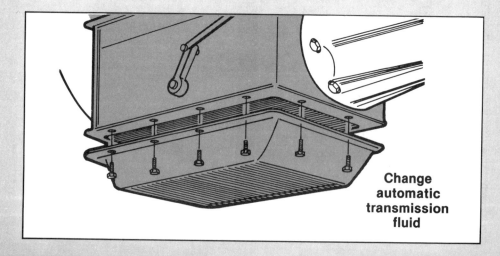

Change automatic transmission fluid

15

Clutch and Transmission Service

NOTE: This chapter describes service procedures that can be done without removing the transmission. Removal of the transmission is a complex procedure requiring special equipment. It should be undertaken only by a professional mechanic.

1 **Check transmission lubricant level.** On models with manual transmission, the oil level should be checked at least twice a year. On models with automatic transmission, fluid level should be checked at every engine oil change (p. 146)

2 **Change automatic transmission fluid** (ATF) (p. 147). This should be done regularly. Cut the interval in half if your car tows a trailer or is subject to other severe use.

3 **Check automatic transmission linkage adjustment.** Any inaccuracies in the shift linkage adjustment may result in damage to the transmission (p. 148).

4 **Check clutch pedal adjustment.** If the clutch engages very high or very low in the pedal's travel, or if there is gear grinding while shifting, the clutch may need adjustment or replacement (p. 149).

Essential. Basic tools • Safety stands • Rags • Torque wrench • Drain pan • Chocks

• Safety glasses or goggles.
Handy. Hose • Squeeze bottle.

Check lubricant level

DIPSTICK

The transmission fluid in a car with automatic transmission should be checked at every engine oil change. On manual transmissions, the fluid level should be checked at least twice a year.

For automatic transmissions

1 Put the shift lever in the Park position.

2 Locate transmission dipstick. It is on the right (passenger's) side in the rear of the engine compartment.

3 Remove dipstick and wipe clean. Start the engine and allow it to warm up. Insert the dipstick into the transmission as far as it will go.

4 Remove dipstick and shut engine off. Fluid adhering to the dipstick should be warm to the touch. If it isn't, run the engine again until it is warm.

5 Read the fluid level on the dipstick. The fluid level should be no lower than 1/4 inch below the ADD mark on the dipstick.

6 Add transmission fluid if level is low. ATF (Dexron II) is added to the automatic transmission through the dipstick tube. It is necessary to use a funnel with a long neck to add fluid. *CAUTION: Do not overfill. It takes only one pint*

to raise the fluid level from ADD to FULL on the dipstick.

7 Start engine and retest fluid level. Add more fluid if necessary.

For manual transmissions

1 Chock the rear wheels. Raise the front of the car and support it on safety stands. Set parking brake.

2 Locate the transmission filler plug. It is on the right (passenger's) side of the transmission.

3 Remove the filler plug with an open end wrench. Insert your finger into the hole to check the lubricant level. If you can feel the oil near the edge of the hole, the level is OK. If you cannot feel oil, then the level is low.

4 Add 80W-90 GL5 gear oil to 3- and 4-speed transmissions. Add Dexron II automatic transmission fluid to 5-speed transmissions.

Note: The oil will flow faster if it is at room temperature (70°F). Fill to the edge of the hole.

5 Clean the filler plug and reinstall it.

Change automatic transmission fluid

This job should be performed regularly. The transmission oil filter should be changed at the same time. The filter can be purchased in a kit along with the proper filter gasket or seal and oil pan gasket.

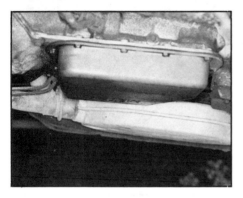

Changing the automatic transmission fluid involves removing the transmission oil pan. This cannot be done by the do-it-yourselfer on all models. Before attempting to remove the oil pan, check the retaining bolts to be sure they are accessible. On some models the rear cross-member must be removed to gain access to the oil pan retaining bolts. This could be a dangerous job. Leave it to a professional mechanic.

1 Chock rear wheels. Raise the front of the car and support it on safety stands. Set parking brake.

2 Start the engine and let it run until it is warm.

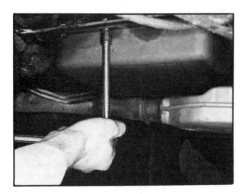

3 Place a pan under the transmission. Remove the drain plug from the transmission oil pan and allow the ATF to drain.

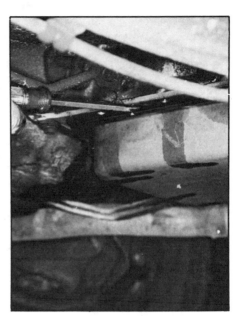

OR if your transmission oil pan is not equipped with a drain plug, remove the attaching bolts from the front and side of the pan and loosen the rear attaching bolts approximately four turns. Loosen the transmission pan gently with a screwdriver. This will allow the fluid to drain.

Note: This can be a messy job. Be prepared with plenty of rags and a large drain pan.

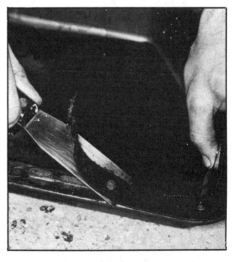

4 Remove oil pan retaining bolts. Remove oil pan. Remove and discard the gasket.

5 Drain remaining fluid from oil pan. Clean oil pan and gasket area on the transmission.

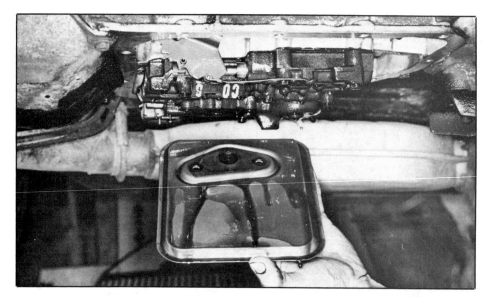

6 Remove the two retaining screws from the filter. Remove the filter, noting its position to facilitate installing the new filter.

7 Install new filter, screwing in the two retaining screws. Be sure the filter gasket or seal is installed between filter and filter mounting surface.

Note: No sealer is required on this gasket.

8 Install new oil pan gasket on the oil pan. Sealer may be used to secure gasket to oil pan.

9 Install oil pan on transmission. Start several bolts to hold pan in place. Install all oil pan bolts. Torque to 12 foot-pounds.

10 Lower car. Add three quarts of ATF (Dexron II) to transmission using the procedure outlined under "Check fluid level."

11 Start engine and let it idle. With parking brake set, move shift selector through all gears including Reverse, then set it in Park. Check fluid level. Add more fluid as necessary.

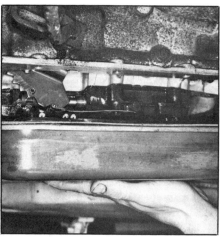

Note: You may have to add up to one or two quarts more.

Check automatic transmission linkage adjustment

Linkage adjustment is critical to proper operation of the transmission. If you find that adjustment is needed, take your car to a professional mechanic.

1 Turn ignition key to ON. Set parking brake.

2 Move the shift lever to Drive. Do not use the pointer as a reference, but position the lever by counting the detents (locating notches inside the transmission). Drive is the third

detent from Park.

3 The shift lever should now be inhibited from engaging in Low unless it is manually released. On column shifters this is done by pulling the shift lever towards the steering wheel. On console shifters this is done by depressing the button on the center of the shift lever.

4 Put the shift lever in Neutral by counting

the transmission detents. Neutral is one detent from Drive in the direction of Park. The lever should now be inhibited from engaging in Reverse unless it is manually released. A properly adjusted linkage will prevent the shift lever from moving beyond both Neutral and Drive unless the lever is manually released as described in the preceding steps.

5 If you feel adjustment is required, see a professional mechanic.

Check clutch pedal

You should adjust the clutch pedal if the gears are grinding or if your car doesn't begin to move until the clutch pedal is almost at the top of its travel.

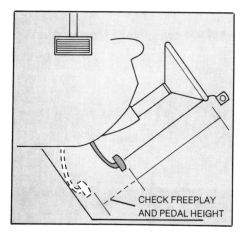

CHECK FREEPLAY AND PEDAL HEIGHT

1 With the engine running, the transmission in Neutral, and your foot off the clutch pedal, depress the pedal lightly with your hand to feel for free play, which should be at least an inch. If there is no free play, suspect a clutch that is too tightly adjusted (free play decreases as the clutch wears). To confirm this, step on the clutch (with the hand brake on) and put the transmission in gear. Slowly release the clutch pedal and, when the engine begins to labor, note how high the clutch pedal has traveled. If it came almost all the way up before the engine began to labor, then you can be sure there is not enough free play, and the clutch must be adjusted. A symptom of this condition might be poor gas mileage and, in severe cases, a burning smell. If this condition is not corrected, the clutch will probably burn out. In some cases, your clutch may be too worn out to adjust and you will have to replace it.

2 If there is too much play in the clutch (this can be determined by depressing the

clutch pedal and not feeling any resistance, except that of the pedal return spring, until the pedal is almost to the floor) and there is a grinding sound when you attempt to put the transmission into gear, then you can be sure your clutch needs adjustment. If this condition is not corrected you will probably damage the transmission synchronizers and gears.

To adjust clutch pedal on all models except Astre and Sunbird

On some Pontiacs, it is possible to reach the adjustment nut from under the hood, while with others you'll have to raise the front of the car and support it on safety stands. You may also have to jack up and support the rear of the car to give you ample room to work.

1 Disconnect the return spring at the clutch fork.

2 Remove the clutch pushrod from its hole in the clutch lever and install it in the gauge hole (above the "working" hole).

3 Push the clutch lever as far forward as you can, then push the clutch fork rearward until you feel firm resistance.

4 Loosen the pushrod lock nut and screw the rod in or out of its threaded collar until it just fits between the clutch lever and the clutch fork with no clearance.

5 Remove the pushrod from the gauge hole and reinstall it in the "working" hole.

6 Reconnect the return spring.

7 Check to see that the pedal free play is one to one and a half inches.

Note: Some early models have no gauge hole. In these cases, simply shorten or lengthen the pushrod until the proper pedal free play is achieved.

8 If after adjusting the clutch pedal, there is grinding while shifting, or if the clutch pedal is very high or low, the clutch may need replacement. See a professional mechanic.

To adjust clutch on Astre/Sunbird

Note: The Astre and Sunbird use a cable-actuated clutch.

1 Remove the ball stud cap and loosen the lock nut on ball stud end located to the right (passenger's) side of the transmission on the clutch housing.

2 Turn the ball stud to obtain one inch of pedal free play.

3 Tighten the lock nut without changing the adjustment, then install the ball stud cap.

4 Depress the pedal several times and recheck free play.

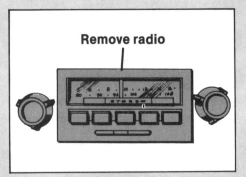

Remove radio

Replace fuses

ELECTRICAL

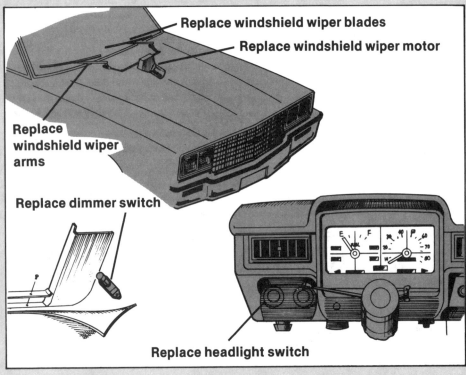

Replace windshield wiper blades

Replace windshield wiper motor

Replace windshield wiper arms

Replace dimmer switch

Replace headlight switch

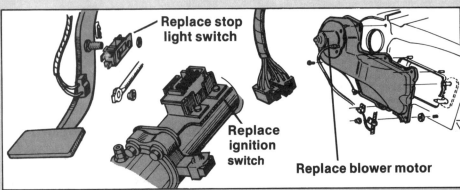

Replace stop light switch

Replace ignition switch

Replace blower motor

16

Electrical System Service

1 **Remove radio.** If your radio has been blowing fuses or has other problems, it may need service. You can save some of the repair costs by removing the radio yourself and taking it to a radio shop (p. 152).

2 **Replace windshield wiper blades.** Your car may have one of two types of blades: the bayonet or the side saddle pin. You can replace both types (p.153). You can also replace the rubber inserts (p. 153).

3 **Replace windshield wiper arms.** They are easy to remove and replace, but follow the procedure carefully to avoid scratching the windshield or breaking the pivot arm (p. 153).

4 **Replace windshield wiper motor.** If the wiper motor stops working and the problem is in the electrical system, see a professional mechanic. But if it's only a defective wiper motor, you can replace it yourself (p. 154).

5 **Replace headlight switch.** You may have to remove this switch to get at another component or to replace the switch itself (p. 155).

6 **Replace dimmer switch.** Replacement may be necessary if either the upper or lower light beams are not working (p. 156).

7 **Replace stop light switch.** Your brake lights won't work if this switch is defective (p. 156).

8 **Replace blower motor.** When you turn on your ventilating system and there is no movement of air, your blower may be defective (p. 157).

9 **Replace fuses.** When an electrical circuit fails, check the fuse block under the dash (p. 157).

Essential. Basic tools.

Remove radio

If your radio has been blowing fuses or has other problems, chances are it will have to come out for repair. You can save a big part of the total repair cost by removing it yourself and taking it to the radio shop.

1 Disconnect the battery ground cable.

2 Remove the control knobs. On some models, it is necessary to push in on the metal retainer located in the slot at the base of the knob.

3 Remove the bezels.

4 Using a deep socket, remove the control shaft nuts and washers.

5 On air-conditioned cars, it may be necessary to remove the lap cooler duct.

6 Remove the radio support nuts or bolts.

7 Disconnect the antenna lead and the speaker and feed wires.

8 Push the radio forward and lower it from the dash.

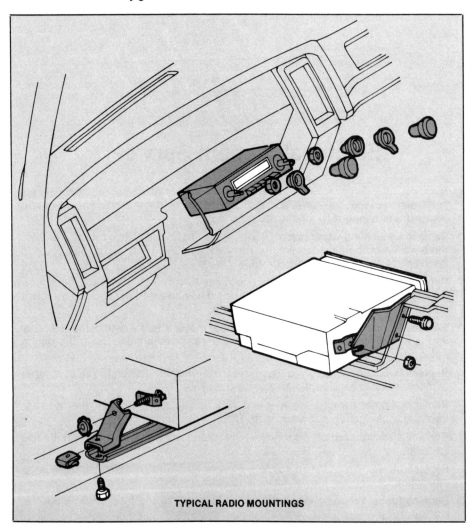

TYPICAL RADIO MOUNTINGS

Replace windshield wiper blades

Your car may have either bayonet or side saddle pin wiper blades.

To replace a bayonet blade

1 To remove a Trico-manufactured blade, press down on the arm to unlock the stop stud, depress the tab on the saddle, and pull the blade from the arm. To remove an Anco-manufactured blade, press inward on the tab and pull the blade from the arm.

2 To install a new blade assembly, slide the blade saddle over the end of the wiper arm so that the locking stud snaps into place.

To replace a side saddle pin blade

1 To remove the blade, insert a screwdriver into the spring release opening of the blade saddle, depress the spring clip, and pull the blade from the arm.

2 To install a new blade, push the blade saddle onto the pin so that the spring clip engages it.

To replace the rubber element

1 To remove a Trico-manufactured blade, squeeze the latch lock release and pull the element out of the lever jaws. To remove an Anco-manufactured blade, depress the latch pin and slide the element out of the yoke jaws.

2 To install the new element, insert it through the yoke or lever jaws, making sure it is fully engaged at all points.

Replace windshield wiper arms

1 Swing the arm-and-blade assembly away from the windshield.

2 Unlock any latch clips or articulating arm clips that may be present.

3 Hold the assembly in this position and pull the arm off the pivot shaft with a removal tool or pry it off carefully using a screwdriver with a wide blade.

4 To install new wiper arms, hold the arm and blade in the swing-out position and push the arm onto the pivot shaft. Make sure the arm parks in the proper position.

TOOL

WIPER PIVOT

Replace windshield wiper motor

If the wiper motor stops working, the cause may be an open circuit breaker or a blown fuse, a break in the wiring, a faulty switch or motor, bent or damaged linkage, or an inoperative governor on the intermittent wiper system. Take the car to a professional mechanic, and if he pinpoints the problem as anything other than a faulty motor, let him do the repair. If the problem is in the motor, however, you can replace it yourself. Buying a used one from a wrecking yard will save money. The wiper motor is located under the hood on the firewall.

1 Make sure the wipers are in the parked position.

2 Disconnect the battery ground cable.

3 Remove the electrical connections and the washer hoses from the motor assembly.

4 Remove the plastic access cover or the plenum chamber grill, depending on the model.

5 Remove the motor-to-linkage nuts.

6 Remove the motor retaining screws or nuts and remove the motor.

7 To replace wiper motor, reverse the procedure.

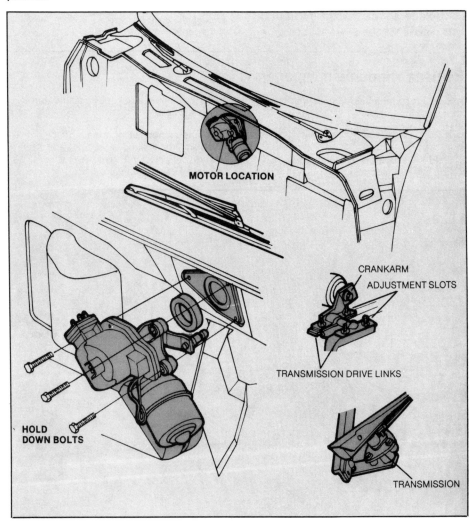

MOTOR LOCATION

CRANKARM

ADJUSTMENT SLOTS

TRANSMISSION DRIVE LINKS

HOLD DOWN BOLTS

TRANSMISSION

Replace headlight switch

You may have to remove the headlight switch to get at another component or to replace the switch itself.

1 Disconnect the battery ground cable.

2 Pull the headlight control knob to the ON position.

3 Reach up under the dash and press the switch shaft release button on the switch and pull out the shaft. It may be necessary to remove a lower dash panel to reach the switch.

Note: On some 1978-80 models, remove the knob from the shaft rather than the shaft from the switch. Depress the retainer tab behind the knob to remove it.

4 Remove the ferrule nut that holds the switch to the dash.

5 Lower the switch and remove the multi-connector from it. It may be necessary to pry the connector off with a screwdriver.

6 Attach the multi-connector to the new switch and reverse the above procedure.

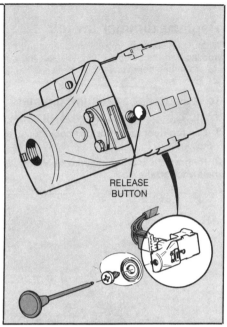

RELEASE BUTTON

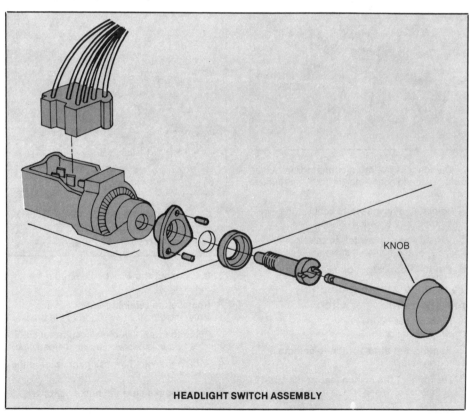

HEADLIGHT SWITCH ASSEMBLY

KNOB

Replace dimmer switch

When your upper or lower light beams are not working and the bulbs are OK, suspect the wiring or the dimmer switch. If the switch is faulty, you can replace it.

To replace floor-mounted dimmer switch

1 Pull the floor carpet or mat back from the switch area.

2 Remove the mounting screws holding the switch to the floor.

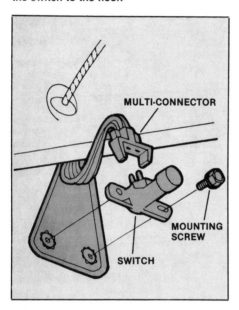

3 Disconnect the multi-connector from the switch by bending the lock fingers out. Remove the switch.

4 To install a new switch, connect the wire connectors to the switch terminal.

5 Attach the new switch to the floor with the screws and tighten it down.

6 Put the floor carpet or mat back in place.

To replace steering-column-mounted dimmer switch

1 Remove the screw holding the switch cover, then the cover.

2 Remove the three switch-to-column attaching screws.

3 Disconnect the switch lead at the lower end of the column and attach a wire to the lead end of the harness.

4 Pull on the switch to draw the harness out of the column.

5 Attach the wire to the new harness, then pull it back down through the column.

6 Reconnect the harness and attach the new switch to the column.

Replace stop light switch

The mechanical switch is installed in a bracket so that its button contacts the brake pedal arm.

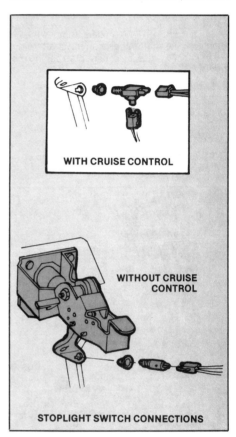

STOPLIGHT SWITCH CONNECTIONS

1 Disconnect the wire harness from the switch connector.

2 Remove the retaining nut or clip and unscrew the stop light switch from the bracket.

3 Place the new switch in the bracket so that the button is depressed with the pedal up.

4 Attach the wire harness connector to the switch.

5 Test to make sure the brake lights are working.

Replace the blower motor

On most models without air conditioning, the blower motor is easily replaced.

1 Disconnect the battery ground cable.

2 Disconnect the blower feed wire at the motor.

3 On some models, it may be necessary to move the inner fender skirt out of the way as follows: Remove the heater hoses and wires that are attached to the fender skirt. Except on Ventura, remove all the fender-skirt attaching bolts except those at the radiator support. On Ventura, remove the eight rearmost fender-skirt attaching screws. Pull out and down on the fender skirt and place a block of wood between the skirt and the fender to allow room to remove the blower motor.

4 On all models, remove the blower-to-case attaching screws.

5 Remove the blower assembly. Pry gently to break the adhesive seal.

6 Remove the blower wheel attaching nut and separate the motor from the wheel.

7 To reinstall a new motor, reverse the above steps, being sure to mount the wheel so that its open end is away from the motor. Make sure the adhesive seal is intact.

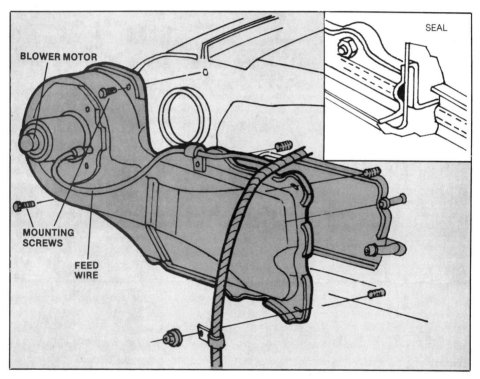

SEAL

BLOWER MOTOR

MOUNTING SCREWS

FEED WIRE

Replace fuses

Should a fuse blow, the cause is usually an overload or short circuit. The fuse panel is located under the dash on a bracket to the left of the steering column. Remove the fuse in question and examine it to see if the thin wire inside the glass tube is broken. Sometimes the glass will appear blackened, which indicates that the fuse has blown. A clamp-type clothespin, which resembles a fuse puller, can easily be modified to pull fuses from the fuse block. Some later models use the miniaturized fusing system. This does a better job in the same space. The fuses themselves have two spade connectors, an easily visible fuse element and their capacity marked in large numbers. If you're in doubt as to whether or not the fuse has blown, remove the suspected fuse from the panel and replace it with one you know is good. Make sure the fuse is of the same size and amperage as the suspect fuse. If the replacement also blows, see a professional mechanic.

DIESELS

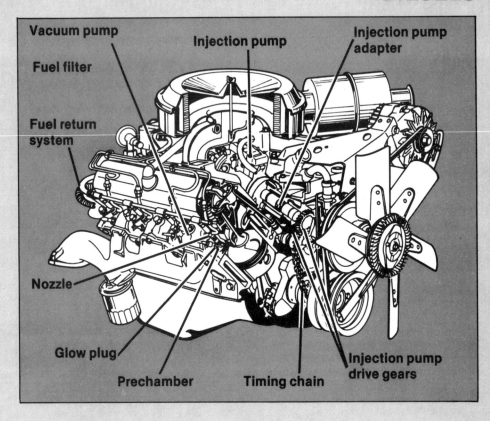

Vacuum pump

Fuel filter

Fuel return system

Injection pump

Injection pump adapter

Nozzle

Glow plug

Prechamber

Timing chain

Injection pump drive gears

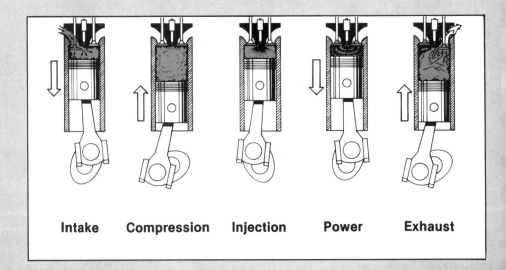

Intake **Compression** **Injection** **Power** **Exhaust**

17

What's different about diesels?

The truck industry's experience with the diesel engine has been very good. Fuel mileage is superb, much routine maintenance (such as ignition tune-up) is eliminated, and, while parts are expensive, their longevity makes up for their high price.

Many of the routine service procedures, tests, and common breakdown repairs on diesels are similar to those performed on cars with conventional gasoline engines. The different service procedures described in this chapter can be performed by the do-it-yourselfer. All diesels are different from gasoline engines in the design and/or function of the cylinder heads, combustion chambers, fuel distribution system, air-intake manifold, and method of ignition. This discussion will outline the service procedures.

How it works

Except for more frequent oil changes, the diesel engine requires little maintenance when compared to the gasoline engine, primarily because it doesn't have the complicated ignition and carburetion systems of the gasoline engine.

The intake stroke of the diesel is similar to the intake stroke of the gasoline engine, except that there is no carburetor to mix fuel with air and no throttle valve to restrict the amount of air entering the cylinder. Therefore, the cylinder fills with air only. When this air becomes compressed, its temperature rises above the ignition point of the fuel. As the piston nears the end of the compression stroke, fuel is injected into the combustion chamber by a fuel-injection system that meters, pressurizes, and distributes fuel to all cylinders. The fuel is ignited by the heat of the compressed air. Since this type of ignition does not require an electrical-spark ignition system, the diesel does not have a distributor, spark plug wires, spark plugs, or high-voltage ignition. In cold weather, tiny electrical heaters called glow plugs heat the precombustion chambers to assist in starting. They remain on for a short time after the engine is started, then turn off when the air in the chamber reaches a temperature high enough to ignite the fuel when it is compressed.

Servicing the V-8 diesel

The diesel engine compares in size with the V-8 gasoline engine, which was the starting point in the engineering of the diesel version. However, the diesel's cylinder block, crankshaft, main bearings, rods, pistons, and pins are of heavier construction because of the higher compression ratio needed to ignite diesel fuel. Further, the GM diesel does not have a catalytic converter or any emission-control devices, except for a crankcase ventilation system.

Before attempting any GM diesel engine maintenance, read these two paragraphs:
(1) Do not clean the engine until it has cooled to surrounding temperature. Spraying water or engine cleaning solvent on the diesel injection pump when it is warm or hot will damage the pump.
(2) The engine has many colored bolts, screws, etc., which are in metric measurement. So be careful when replacing the fasteners. Make sure the replacements have the same measurements and strengths as those removed.

The fuel-injection pump is mounted on top of the diesel engine. The pump provides the required timing advance under all operating conditions. Timing advance is preset at the factory.

The fuel filter is located between the mechanical fuel pump and the injection pump. The diaphragm-type mechanical fuel pump is mounted on the right side of the engine and is driven by a cam on the crankshaft. There is also a fuel filter in the fuel tank.

Because burned diesel fuel leaves behind more by-products than does gasoline, the oil must be changed more frequently in diesels than in gasoline engines. GM recommends that you change

the oil and filter of the V-8 diesel every 3000 miles. Seven quarts are required. Use only oil that says SE/CC on the can.

The injector pump and the injectors themselves are engineered to very close tolerances and are extremely sensitive to the cleanliness of the fuel. Therefore, be certain to change the fuel filter at the recommended intervals.

There are two types of electrical glow plug systems used in GM diesels—both operate off of two 12-volt batteries. One system has two relays (on the firewall near the wiper motor) that activate the 12-volt glow plugs; the other has one relay box (on the right fender filler panel) that activates the 6-volt glow plugs.

Note: 12-volt and 6-volt plugs are not interchangeable, so make sure you know which type your car takes.

CAUTION: The single relay-box system supplies a pulsing current to the glow plugs. Do not bypass or apply electrical current to the relay because you will instantly damage the plugs.

If your diesel is hard to start or runs roughly when cold, test the glow plug system with a voltmeter. With the ignition switch in the RUN position (the WAIT light must be on—otherwise the engine is too warm for the glow plug circuit to be activated), attach the negative lead of the voltmeter to a good ground and touch the positive lead to the glow plug's wire connector. Depending on the type of system your car has, you should see either a steady 12-volt reading or a pulsating 6-volt reading. If there is no voltage at the glow-plug wire, check the feed circuit and relay(s). If there is voltage, remove each glow plug in turn, reattach its lead, turn on the key (again, the WAIT light must be on) and touch the threads of the glow plug to a good ground, holding the plug by its insulated wire connector. The plug should heat up and glow. Replace any plugs that don't. Also, clean any plugs that are heavily coated with carbon.

If you suspect internal engine wear or damage, you can take a compression test at the glow plug holes. A special high-pressure diesel compression gauge must be used because the engine's 22.5:1 compression ratio is far too much for an ordinary gasoline engine gauge to withstand. Also, you must disconnect the wire from the fuel solenoid on the injection pump. Disconnect all the wires from the glow plugs and remove all the plugs.

Crank the engine for at least six puffs. Every cylinder should read at least 275 psi, and the lowest should not be less than 70 percent of the highest. If you do not get these results, the valves, rings, etc. may be faulty, so take your car to a professional mechanic who is qualified to work on diesels.

Overview of the V-8 diesel engine. Note the two 12-volt batteries in parallel up front.

Servicing steps

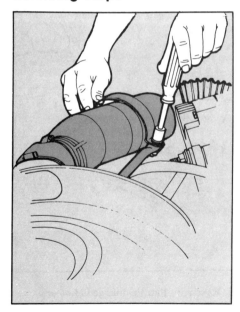

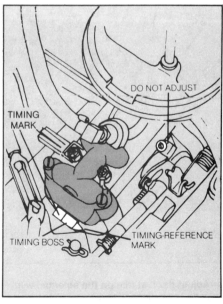

1 Remove the hold-down bolts of the air-intake muffler attached to the air cleaner.

2 Air-intake manifold with air cleaner removed. Timing mark is on the injector, but the timing reference mark is on the engine.

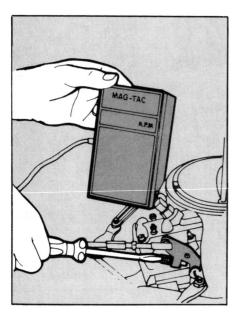

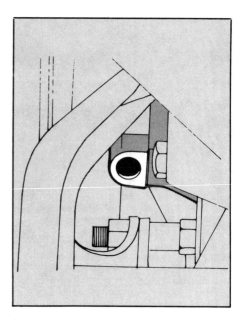

3 Adjust idle speed using a special tachometer, such as the Mag-Tac, a pulse-actuated tachometer with digital readout. This is needed because diesels do not have a spark-type ignition system.

4 The magnetic pulse timing hole is designed to accept the Mag-Tac probe to measure engine speed.

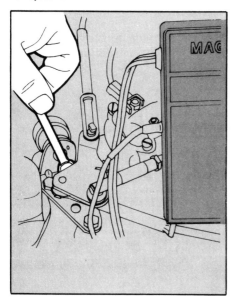

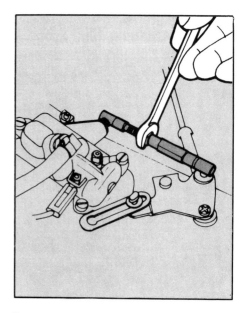

5 Adjust the fast idle on the solenoid with an open-end wrench. Use a Mag-Tac tachometer or equivalent to monitor engine rpm.

6 Make sure throttle linkage is free and properly adjusted.

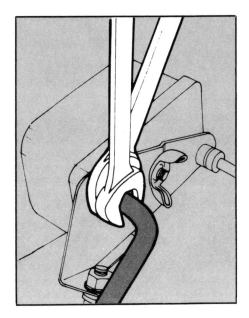

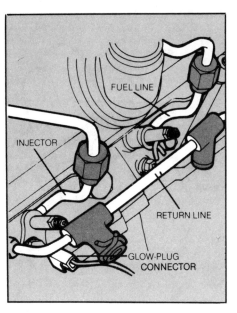

7 **To replace the fuel filter,** the fuel line must first be disconnected. Diesels are very sensitive to the cleanliness of the fuel, so be sure to change the filter regularly.

8 **Each side of the engine has four fuel lines,** four fuel injectors, four glow plugs, four plug connectors, and four fuel return T-fittings.

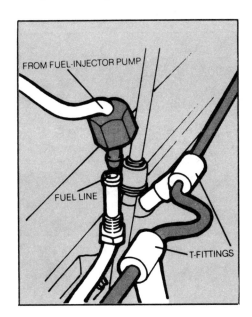

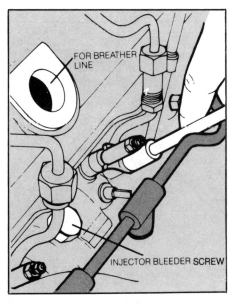

9 **To take out an injector,** first remove the T-fittings by pulling each one up a little at a time in sequence until they come off. Use two wrenches to uncouple the fuel line from the injector.

10 **After the fuel line, return line, and glow plugs** are disconnected, remove the injector retaining cap screw with a socket, extension and ratchet.

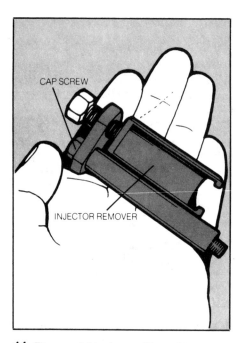

11 **The special tool you will need to remove the fuel injector.**

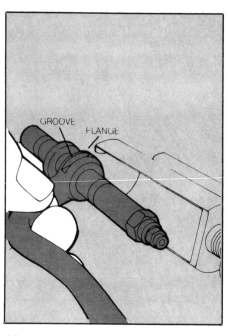

12 **Install the injector removing tool** so the flange of the tool enters the groove on the fuel injector. Lock the injector cap screw before beginning to pull out the injector.

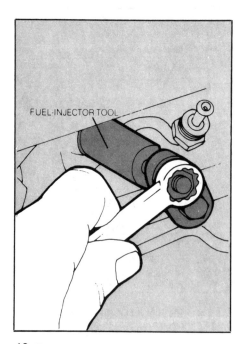

13 **Remove the injector from the engine** with a 9/16-inch closed-end wrench.

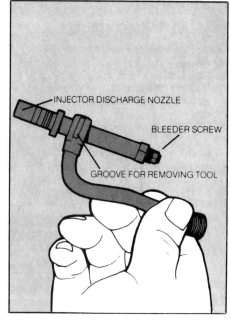

14 **Identify different components of the injector nozzle assembly.**

NEGATIVE VOLTMETER LEAD

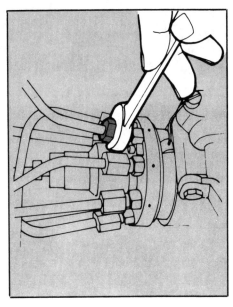

15 **To see if a glow plug is receiving current,** attach a voltmeter, turn the ignition key on, and note the voltage reading (WAIT light must be on).

16 **The fuel injector has as many injector lines as there are cylinders** in the engine. Note the similarity to the ignition wires in a conventional gasoline engine.

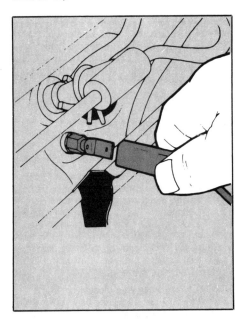

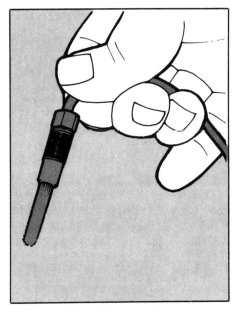

17 **The power connector must be disconnected** from the glow plug before the plug can be removed.

18 **With ignition switch on, connect the glow plug supply line** to each plug and ground the plug. If it doesn't glow, check plug power circuit for continuity. If there's voltage but no glow, replace the glow plug.

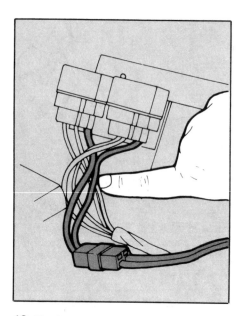

19 The finger points to the wires to be tested when checking a plug that does not glow.

20 To make a compression test, remove a glow plug and install a special high-pressure compression tester in the plug hole. The wire to the injection pump fuel solenoid must be disconnected.

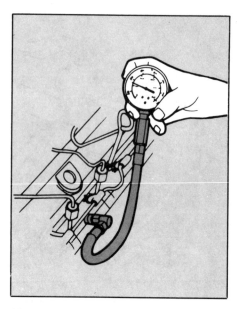

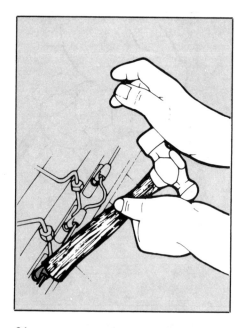

21 After all tests are completed, reassemble the system, reversing the above procedures. A hammer handle will help you to seat the fuel return line.

About diesel fuel. Diesel fuel for vehicles comes in two grades: number 1, which is basically kerosene, and number 2, which is like home heating oil ("stove" oil, however, usually contains more sulphur than is recommended for use in engines).

Diesels are sensitive to the quality of their fuel. The first consideration is cleanliness. Water or other impurities in the fuel can cause serious problems. That's why servicing the fuel filter regularly is so important.

Then there is WAP (Wax Appearance Point), the temperature at which wax crystals begin to form, and they can clog the injection system. Number 1 has a lower WAP than number 2, so it is sometimes used in cold weather. There are, however, two drawbacks to number 1: It doesn't lubricate the pump as well as number 2, and it contains about five percent less energy per gallon.

If wax crystals keep your diesel from starting when the weather is cold, the best remedy is to pull the car into a heated garage until the crystals disappear, then fill the tank with number 1 or winterized number 2. Some experts claim that, in an emergency, a few gallons of gasoline can be added to the tank to keep the WAP down.

Appendix

TUNEUP SPECIFICATIONS: ALL 1970-74 MODELS

The following specifications are published from the latest information available. This data should be used only in the absence of a decal affixed in the engine compartment.

★ When using a timing light, disconnect vacuum hose or tube at distributor and plug opening in hose or tube so idle speed will not be affected.

● When checking compression, lowest cylinder must be within 70% of the highest.

Year & Engine	Spark Plug		Distributor		Ignition Timing BTDC[1] ★	Curb Idle Speed[2]	
	Type	Gap (Inch)	Point Gap (Inch)	Dwell Angle (Deg.)		Man. Trans.	Auto. Trans.[3]
1970							
6-250 Std. Tr.	R46T	.035	.019	31–34	TDC	750/400	—
6-250 Auto. Tr.	R46T	.035	.019	31–34	4°	—	600/400D
8-350 2 Bar. Carb.	R46S	.035	.016	30	9°	800	650D
8-400 2 Bar. Carb.	R46S	.035	.016	30	9°	800	650D
8-400 4 Bar. Carb.	R45S	.035	.016	30	9°	950	650D
8-400 Ram Air	R44S	.035	.016	30	15°	1000/650	750/500D
8-455	R45S[4]	.035	.016	30	9°	950	650D
1971							
6-250	R46TS	.035	.019	32½	4°	850/550	650/500D
8-307 Std. Tr.	R45TS	.035	.019	30	4°	550	—
8-307 Auto. Tr.	R45TS	.035	.019	30	8°	—	550D
8-350 2 Bar. Carb.	R47S	.035	.016	30	12°	800	600D
8-400 2 Bar. Carb.	R47S	.035	.016	30	8°	—	600D
8-400 4 Bar. Carb.	R46S	.035	.016	30	12°	1000/600	700D
8-455	R46S	.035	.016	30	12°	—	650D
8-455 H.O.	R46S	.035	.016	30	12°	1000/600	700D

Year & Engine	Spark Plug		Distributor		Ignition Timing BTDC[1]★	Curb Idle Speed[2]	
	Type	Gap (Inch)	Point Gap (Inch)	Dwell Angle (Deg.)		Man. Trans.	Auto. Trans.[3]

1972

6-250	R46T	.035	.019	32½	4°	850/450	650/450D
8-307 Std. Tr.	R44T	.035	.016	30	4°	900/450	—
8-307 Auto. Tr.	R44T	.035	.016	30	8°	—	600/450D
8-350	R46TS	.035	.016	30	8°	800	—
8-350	R46TS	.035	.016	30	10°	—	625D
8-400 2 Bar. Carb.	R46TS	.035	.016	30	10°	—	625D
8-400 4 Bar. Carb.	R45TS	.035	.016	30	10°	1000/600	700/500D
8-455 2 Bar. Carb.	R45TS	.035	.016	30	10°	—	625D
8-455 4 Bar. Carb.	R45TS	.035	.016	30	10°	—	650/500D
8-455 H.O. Std. Tr.	R45TS	.035	.016	30	8°	1000/600	—
8-455 H.O. Auto. Tr.	R45TS	.035	.016	30	10°	—	700/500D

1973

6-250	R46T	.035	[5]	32½	6°	700/450	600D
V8-350 Std. Tra.	R46TS	.040	.016	30	10°	900/600	—
V8-350 Auto. Tra.	R46TS	.040	.016	30	12°	—	650D
V8-400 2 Bar. Carb.	R46TS	.040	.016	30	[6]	—	650D
V8-400 4 Bar. Carb.	R45TS	.040	.016	30	[6]	1000/600	650D
V8-455	R45TS	.040	.016	30	[6]	1000	650D
V8-455 S.D.	R44TS	.040	.016	30	[6]	1000/600	750/500D

| Year & Engine | Spark Plug | | Distributor | | Ignition Timing BTDC[1] ★ | Curb Idle Speed[2] | |
	Type	Gap (Inch)	Point Gap (Inch)	Dwell Angle (Deg.)		Man. Trans.	Auto. Trans.[3]
1974							
6-250	R46T	.035	[5]	32½	6°	850	600D
V8-350 2 Bar. Carb.[7]	R46TS	.040	[5]	30	[6]	900	650D
V8-350 2 Bar. Carb.[8]	R46TS	.040	[5]	30	10°	—	625D
V8-350 4 Bar. Carb.[7]	R46TS	.040	[5]	30	[6]	—	625D
V8-350 4 Bar. Carb.[8]	R46TS	.040	[5]	30	10°	1000	650D
V8-400 2 Bar. Carb.[7]	R46TS	.040	[5]	30	[6]	—	650D
V8-400 2 Bar. Carb.[8]	R46TS	.040	[5]	30	10°	—	625D
V8-400 4 Bar. Carb.[7]	R45TS	.040	[5]	30	[6]	1000	650D
V8-400 4 Bar. Carb.[8]	R45TS	.040	[5]	30	10°	—	625D
V8-455[7]	R45TS	.040	[5]	30	[6]	—	650D
V8-455[8]	R45TS	.040	[5]	30	10°	—	625D
V8-455 S.D.	R44TS	.040	[5]	30	12°	1000	750D

[1]—BTDC: Before top dead center.
[2]—Where two figures are given, the higher is with solenoid activated.
[3]—D: Drive.
[4]—Use R44S on Ram Air option.
[5]—New points, .019"; used points, .016".
[6]—Man. trans., 10°BTDC; auto. trans., 12°BTDC.
[7]—Except Calif.
[8]—California.

TUNEUP SPECIFICATIONS:
ALL 1975-80 MODELS EXCEPT ASTRE, SUNBIRD AND 1980 PHOENIX

The following specifications are published from the latest information available. This data should be used only in the absence of a decal affixed in the engine compartment.

★ When using a timing light, disconnect vacuum hose or tube at distributor and plug opening in hose or tube so idle speed will not be affected.
● When checking compression, lowest cylinder must be within 70% of the highest.

| Year & Engine | Spark Plug | | Ignition Timing BTDC[1] ★ | | Curb Idle Speed[2] | |
	Type	Gap	Man. Trans.	Auto. Trans.	Man. Trans.	Auto. Trans.
1975						
6-250	R46TX	.060	10°	10°	425/850	[3]
V8-260 Exc. Calif.	R46SX	.080	16°[4]	18°[4]	750	550/650D
V8-260 Calif.	R46SX	.080	—	16°[4]	—	600/650D
V8-350 Ventura	R45TSX	.060	—	12°	—	600D
V8-350 2 Barrel Exc. Ventura	R46TSX	.060	—	16°	—	600D
V8-350 4 Barrel Exc. Calif.[5]	R46TSX	.060	12°	16°	775	650D
V8-350 4 Barrel Calif.[5]	R46TSX	.060	12°	12°	775	625D
V8-400 2 Barrel	R46TSX	.060	—	16°	—	650D
V8-400 4 Barrel Exc. Calif.	R45TSX	.060	12°	16°	775	[6]
V8-400 4 Barrel Calif.	R45TSX	.060	12°	12°	775	600D
V8-455 Exc. Calif.	R45TSX	.060	—	16°	—	650D
V8-455 Calif.	R45TSX	.060	—	10°	—	675D

Year & Engine	Spark Plug		Ignition Timing BTDC[1] ★		Curb Idle Speed[2]	
	Type	Gap	Man. Trans.	Auto. Trans.	Man. Trans.	Auto Trans

1976

Year & Engine	Type	Gap	Man. Trans.	Auto. Trans.	Man. Trans.	Auto Trans
6-250	R46TS	.035	6°	10°	850	[7]
V8-260 Exc. Calif.	[8]	[8]	16°[4]	18°[4]	750	550D[9]
V8-260 Calif.	[8]	[8]	14°[4]	[10]	750	600D
V8-350 Ventura	R45TSX	.060	—	12°	—	600D
V8-350 2 Barrel[5]	R46TSX	.060	—	16°	—	550D
V8-350 4 Barrel[5]	R46TSX	.060	—	16°	—	600D
V8-400 2 Barrel	R46TSX	.060	—	16°	—	550D
V8-400 4 Barrel	R45TSX	.060	12°	16°	775	575D
V8-455 Exc. Calif.	R45TSX	.060	16°	16°	775	550D
V8-455 Calif.	R45TSX	.060	—	12°	—	600D

1977

Year & Engine	Type	Gap	Man. Trans.	Auto. Trans.	Man. Trans.	Auto Trans
4-151	R44TSX	.060	14°[11]	14	[12]	[13]
V6-231[14]	[15]	[15]	12°	12°	600/800	600D[16]
V6-231[17]	R46TSX	.060	—	15°	—	600/670D[18]
V8-301	R46TSX	.060	16°	12°	750/850	550/650D
V8-305	R45TS	.045	—	8°	—	500/650D
V8-350[19]	R45TSX	.060	—	16°	—	575/650D
V8-350[20]	R45TS	.045	—	8°	—	[21]
V8-350[22]	R46SZ	.060	—	[23]	—	[24]
V8-400	R45TSX	.060	18°	[25]	775	[26]
V8-403 Exc. Calif. & High Alt.	R46SZ	.060	—	22°[4]	—	550/650D
V8-403 Calif. & High Alt.	R46SZ	.060	—	20°[4]	—	[27]

1978

Year & Engine	Type	Gap	Man. Trans.	Auto. Trans.	Man. Trans.	Auto Trans
4-151	R43TSX	.060	—	14°[11]	—	[28]
V6-231	R46TSX	.060	15°	15°	800	[29]

Year & Engine	Spark Plug		Ignition Timing BTDC[1] ★		Curb Idle Speed[2]	
	Type	Gap	Man. Trans.	Auto. Trans.	Man. Trans.	Auto Trans
V8-301 2 Barrel	R46TSX	.060	—	12°	—	550/650D
V8-301 4 Barrel	R45TSX	.060	—	12°	—	550/650D
V8-305 Exc. Calif. & High Alt.	R45TS	.045	4°	4°	600/700	500/600D
V8-305 Calif.	R45TS	.045	—	6°	—	500/600D
V8-305 High Alt.	R45TS	.045	—	8°	—	600/700D
V8-350[20]	R45TS	.045	6°	8°	700	[30]
V8-350[22]	R46SZ	.060	—	20°[4]	—	550/650D
V8-350[31]	R46TSX	.060	—	15°	—	550D
V8-400	R45TSX	.060	16°	[25]	775	[26]
V8-403	R46SZ	.060	—	20°[4]	—	[24]

1979

Year & Engine	Spark Plug		Ignition Timing BTDC[1] ★		Curb Idle Speed[2]	
	Type	Gap	Man. Trans.	Auto. Trans.	Man. Trans.	Auto Trans
V6-231	R46TSX	.060	15°	15°	600/800	[32]
V8-301 2 Barrel	R46TSX	.060	—	12°	—	500/650D
V8-301 4 Barrel	R45TSX	.060	14°	12°	700/800	500/650D
V8-305 2 Barrel Exc. Calif.	R45TS	.045	4°	4°	600/700	500/600D
V8-305 2 Barrel Calif.	R45TS	.045	—	4°	—	600/650D
V8-305 4 Barrel	R45TS	.045	—	4°	—	500/6008
V8-350[20]	R45TS	.045	—	8°	—	[30]
V8-350[22]	R46SZ	.060	—	20°[4]	—	500/600D
V8-350[31]	R46TSX	.060	—	15°	—	550D
V8-400	R45TSX	.060	18°	—	775	—
V8-403	R46SZ	.060	—	20°[4]	—	500/600D

Year & Engine	Spark Plug		Ignition Timing BTDC[1] ★		Curb Idle Speed[2]	
	Type	Gap	Man. Trans.	Auto. Trans.	Man. Trans.	Auto Trans

1980

Year & Engine	Type	Gap	Man. Trans.	Auto. Trans.	Man. Trans.	Auto Trans
V6-229 Exc. Calif.	R45TS	.045	—	10°	—	600/670D
V6-231 Exc. Calif.	R45TS	.040	15°	15°	600/800	550/670D
V6-231 Calif.	—	—	—	—	—	—
V8-265	R45TSX	.060	—	10°	—	525/625D
V8-301[33]	R45TSX	.060	—	12°	—	500/650D
V8-301[34]	R45TSX	.060	—	12°	—	550/650D
V8-301[35]	R45TSX	.060	—	8°	—	600/650D
V8-305	R45TS	.045	—	4°	—	550/650D
V8-350 Exc. Calif.[31]	R45TSX	.060	—	15°	—	[32]
V8-350 Calif.[22]	R46SX	.080	—	18°[4]	—	550/650D
V8-350 Diesel	—	—	—	—	—	575-750D

[1]—BTDC—Before top dead center.
[2]—Idle speed on man. trans. vehicles is adjusted in Neutral & on auto. trans. equipped vehicles is adjusted in Drive unless otherwise specified. Where two idle speeds are listed, the higher speed is with the A/C or idle solenoid energized.
[3]—Except Calif., 425/500D RPM; California, 425/600D RPM.
[4]—At 1100 RPM.
[5]—Except Ventura.

[6]—Except full size sta. wag., 650D RPM; full size sta. wag., 625D RPM.
[7]—Except Calif., LeMans with A/C 575D RPM, all other models 550D RPM; California, 600D RPM.
[8]—Early models use R46SX gapped at .080"; late models use R46SZ gapped at .060".
[9]—On Grand LeMans & LeMans models, set to 575D RPM.
[10]—Engine codes TE, TJ, T4 & T5, set to 14° BTDC at 1100 RPM; engine codes TP, TT, T2 & T3, set to 16° BTDC at 1100 RPM.
[11]—At 1000 RPM.
[12]—Less A/C, 500/1000 RPM; with A/C, 500/1200 RPM.
[13]—Less A/C 500/650D RPM; with A/C, 650/850 RPM.
[14]—Except Even-Fire engine.
[15]—R46TS gapped at .040" or R46TSX gapped at .060".
[16]—On Ventura, Phoenix & full size models with A/C, set to 600/670D RPM.
[17]—Even-Fire engine.
[18]—On full size models, idle speed with solenoid energized is set with A/C on.
[19]—Distributor located rear of engine, rotor rotation counter clockwise. Fuel pump located left side of engine.
[20]—Distributor located rear of engine, rotor rotation clockwise.
[21]—Except high altitude 500/650D RPM; high altitude, 600/650 RPM.
[22]—Distributor located rear of engine, rotor rotation counter clockwise. Fuel located right side of engine.
[23]—Except Firebird, Phoenix & Ventura Calif. models, 20° BTDC at 1100 RPM; Firebird, Phoenix & Ventura California models, 18° BTDC at 1100 RPM.
[24]—Except high altitude, 550/650D RPM; high altitude, 600/700D RPM.
[25]—Except Firebird high performance engine (engine code Y6), 16° BTDC; Firebird high performance engine (engine code Y6), 18° BTDC.
[26]—Except Firebird high performance engine (engine code Y6), 575/650D RPM; Firebird high performance engine (engine code Y6), 600/700D RPM.
[27]—Except high altitude, 550/650D RPM; high altitude, 600/650D RPM.
[28]—Less A/C, 500/650D RPM: with A/C, 650/850D RPM.
[29]—Less idle solenoid, 600D RPM; with idle solenoid, 600/670D RPM.
[30]—Except high altitude, 500/600D RPM; high altitude, 600/650D RPM.
[31]—Distributor located at front of engine.
[32]—Less idle solenoid, 600D RPM; with idle solenoid, 550/670D RPM.
[33]—Except E/C (electronic control) & turbocharged engines.
[34]—E/C (electronic control) engine.
[35]—Turbocharged engine.

TUNEUP SPECIFICATIONS: ASTRE AND SUNBIRD

The following specifications are published from the latest information available. This data should be used only in the absence of a decal affixed in the engine compartment.

★ When using a timing light, disconnect vacuum hose or tube at distributor and plug opening in hose or tube so idle speed will not be affected.

● When checking compression, lowest cylinder must be within 70 percent of highest.

Year & Engine	Spark Plug		Ignition Timing BTDC[1] ★		Curb Idle Speed[2]	
	Type	Gap	Man. Trans.	Auto. Trans.	Man. Trans.	Auto. Trans.
1975						
4-140 1 Barrel	R43TSX	.060	8°	10°	700/1200	550/750D
4-140 2 Barrel	R43TSX[3]	.060	10°	12°	[4]	600/750D
1976						
4-140 1 Barrel	R43TS	.035	8°	10°	750/1200	650/750D
4-140 2 Barrel Exc. Calif.	R43TS	.035	8°	10°	700[5]	600/750D
4-140 2 Barrel Calif.	R43TS	.035	8°	10°	700/1000	600/750D
V6-231	R44SX	.060	12°	12°	600/800	600D
1977						
4-140 Exc. Calif. & High Alt.	R43TS	.035	TDC	2°	700/1250	650/850D
4-140 Calif.	R43TS	.035	[6]	TDC	800/1250	650/850D
4-140 High Alt.	R43TS	.035	TDC	2°	800/1250	700/850D
4-151 Exc. Calif.	R44TSX	.060	14°[7]	14°	[8]	[9]
4-151 Calif.	R44TSX	.060	—	12°	—	[9]
V6-231[10]	[11]	[11]	12°	12°	600/800	600D
V6-231[12]	R46TSX	.060	—	15°	—	600/670D
1978						
4-151 Exc. Calif.	R43TSX	.060	14°[7]	12°[7]	[13]	[9]
4-151 Calif.	R43TSX	.060	—	14°[7]	—	[9]
V6-231	R46TSX	.060	15°	15°	600/800	600/670D
V8-305 Exc. Calif. & High Alt.	R45TS	.045	4°	4°	600	500D
V8-305 Calif.	R45TS	.045	—	6°	—	500D
V8-305 High Alt.	R45TS	.045	—	8°	—	600D

Year & Engine	Spark Plug		Ignition Timing BTDC[1] ★		Curb Idle Speed[2]	
	Type	Gap	Man. Trans.	Auto. Trans.	Man. Trans.	Auto Trans
1979						
4-151 Exc. Calif.	R43TSX	.060	12°	12°	[14]	[9]
4-151 Calif.	R43TSX	.060	14°[7]	14°[7]	1000/1200	[9]
V6-231	[15]	.060	15°	15°	600/800	[16]
V8-305 Exc. Calif.	R45TS	.045	4°	4°	600	500/600D
V8-305 Calif.	R45TS	.045	—	2°	—	600/650D
1980						
4-151 Exc. Calif.	R44TSX	.060	12°	12°	[17]	[18]
4-151 Calif.	R44TSX	.060	14°	14°	[19]	[18]
V6-231 Exc. Calif.	**R45TSX**	.060	15°	15°	600/800	[20]
V6-231 Calif.	R45TSX	.060	15°	15°	800	[21]

[1]—BTDC—Before top dead center.
[2]—Idle speed on man. trans. vehicles is adjusted in Neutral & on auto. trans. equipped vehicles is adjusted in Drive unless otherwise specified. Where two idle speeds are listed, the higher speed is with the A/C or idle solenoid energized.
[3]—If cold weather starting problems are encountered, use R43TS spark plug gapped at .035″.
[4]—Except Calif., 700 RPM; Calif., 700/1200 RPM.
[5]—With A/C override switch disconnected & A/C on, solenoid is adjusted to 1200 RPM in Neutral.
[6]—2°ATDC, after top dead center.
[7]—At 1000 RPM.
[8]—Less A/C, 500/1000 RPM; with A/C, 500/1200 RPM.
[9]—Less A/C, 500/650D RPM; with A/C, 650/850D RPM.
[10]—Except even fire engine.
[11]—On early models, use R46TS gapped at .040″; on late models, use R46TSX gapped at .060″.
[12]—Even fire engine.
[13]—Less A/C, 500/1000 RPM; with A/C, 900/1200 RPM.
[14]—Less A/C, 500/900 RPM; with A/C, 900/1250 RPM.
[15]—R45TSX or R46TSX.
[16]—Less idle solenoid, 600D RPM; with idle solenoid, 550/670D RPM.
[17]—Less A/C, 550/1000 RPM; with A/C, 1000/1250 RPM.
[18]—Less A/C, 550/650D RPM; with A/C, 650/850D RPM.
[19]—Less A/C, 500/1000 RPM; with A/C, 1000/1200 RPM.
[20]—Less idle solenoid, 550D RPM; with idle solenoid, 550/670D RPM.
[21]—Less idle solenoid, 550D RPM; with idle solenoid, 550/620D RPM.

Tire Sizes

The profile ratio of a tire is the relation of it's cross-section height, from tread to bead, compared to its cross-section width, from sidewall to sidewall. A 70-series tire, for example, has a profile ratio of 70, that is, the height of the tire is 70 percent of the width.

For many years, a profile ratio of approximately 83 was considered standard or conventional for most bias-ply passenger car tires. With the advent of bias-belted and radial-ply constructions, lower profile tires with ratios of 78, 70, and even 60 have become popular. Today, most new cars are equipped with 70- or 78-series tires.

Both tire construction and profile ratio can have a pronounced influence on the handling and performance characteristics of a car. In selecting new tires, therefore, it is advisable first to check the manufacturer's specifications in the owner's manual.

Prior to 1967, common tire size designations consisted of numbers, such as 7.75-14 or 9.50-15. In numerical designations, the first number (7.75) refers to the approximate cross-section width in inches of an inflated tire, and the second number (14) is the rim diameter. Tires with numerical size designations have an 83 profile ratio and are all but obsolete except on second line economy tires.

With the advent of wider profile ratios in 1967, a new series of size designations using letters and numbers went into effect. Tires from 78-series through 50-series use the letters A through N to identify size, with A being the smallest tire and N the largest. The letter is followed by a number to indicate the tire's approximate height-to-width ratio, followed by the rim diameter. For instance, on an F78-14 tire, the number 78 means that the tire is 78 percent as high as it is wide. The number 14 indicates that it fits a 14-inch rim. Radial tire manufacturers use several size designations. One uses a combination of metric and inch designations. In the case of a 195 R 14 size, for example, the number 195 refers to the approximate cross-section width in millimeters. R means radial and 14 is the rim diameter in inches. Radials of the 78, 70, 60, and 50-series use the same size designations as their bias-ply or bias-belted equivalents with the addition of the letter R.

Even this letter designation system is not universally accepted. Some companies are using a metric system to designate a 70-series tire. So you might see a tire marked 185 70-13. This identifies a 70-series tire that is equivalent to the old 185 metric size.

Other tire markings

You might see a tire marked GR70VR-15. This tire fits on a 15-inch rim and it is a 70-series radial, size G. The V is a speed designation. There are three letters used to indicate at what maximum speed a tire is safe. A tire marked S is good for up to 113 miles per hour; a tire marked H is good to 130; and a tire marked V is safe to 165 miles per hour. These designations are given after a tire is operated at that speed for 24 hours under a full load.

Sidewall markings

P metric tires were introduced into the marketplace during 1977 and are now furnished as original equipment on a number of cars.

Alpha-numeric tire size designations have been in widespread use in the US for some time (an example: the FR78-14). In addition, there are a number of older designations for European metric tires, mostly on imports (an example: the 195R14).

The P series metric tire size designations are set up as explained in the following example:

P 205/75R14

P identifies passenger car tire

205 is the width in millimeters (one millimeter ⅔ .04 inch)

75 is the height-to-width ratio

R identifies radial construction (B if bias-belted or D if diagonal or bias)

14 is the rim diameter in inches

While these tires are designed in terms of kilograms (kg) for load and kilopascals (kPa) for inflation, tire sidewall labeling will also show loads in pounds and inflation in psi.

There are several important considerations when replacing one of the above types with the other. The most important of these are: load and inflation, dimensions, and construction type.

Tire load and inflation pressure are closely related. Because of different load and inflation relationships of P series metric and standard sizes, they are not exactly interchangeable.

A replacement tire must have an adequate capacity to carry the maximum load for which the car was designed. Consult the vehicle tire information placard to find the recommended original equipment tire size(s) and recommended inflation pressures, from which you can find the corresponding tire load. The placard is usually located on the driver's doorpost or on the glove box door. Select a replacement tire size which has a load-carrying capacity equal to or greater than the original tire size at the highest similar inflation pressure.

You may use a replacement tire with slightly less load capacity (at the pressure referred to above for the original tire) by adjusting its inflation pressure to obtain the necessary load capacity.

The load capacity of the replacement tire at the new adjusted inflation pressure must always equal or exceed the load capacity of the original equipment tire at its recommended inflation pressure. Never exceed the maximum permissible inflation pressure shown on the replacement tire sidewall.

Make sure the new tire fits properly on the car and does not rub or cause changes in steering. Clearance should be checked through suspension travel.

As a general rule, do not mix different sizes on the same axle. However, you may mount tires of different sizes on the same axle when construction, dimensions, and load capacity are compatible. Consult the tire manufacturer for specifics on this.

Never mix radial and non-radial tires on the same axle unless you have to use your spare temporarily.

Snow Tires

When radial tires became popular several years ago, many experts said that a radial's traction was so much better than a bias-ply or bias-belted tires that snow tires were no longer necessary.

While it is true that radial tire traction is a vast improvement over that of other tires, even the best radial cannot compare with a real snow tire in snowy conditions. A radial may yield 40 percent of snow tire traction, so if you live in an area where little snow falls, 40 percent may be enough. If, on the other hand, you live where snow falls frequently and heavily, you will probably want to have all the traction you can get and therefore to invest in snow tires.

In extreme weather conditions, even plain snow tires may not be enough. You may have to use studded snow tires or tire chains with snow tires to get you through the winter.

A welded-type chain might be best for occasional use—like a trip to a ski resort. But for everyday use around the city, two or three strap-on chains are more convenient since they can be installed without jacking up the car.

Plain snow tires will not help much on glare ice. However, with either ceramic or tungsten studs buried in the tread, snow tires perform on packed snow or ice almost as well as chains. Since some states strictly limit their use, you would do well to look up the laws governing snow tires before buying them.

Today, snow tires are made with bias-ply, bias-belted, and radial-ply construction, so that you can match your front tires with the right type of snow tire. It is essential that you do so. Otherwise your car will exhibit handling difficulties which could prove dangerous in an emergency. Snow tires are also made in various profile ratios, again to match the type of tire you have on the front of your car. Ideally you would have the same construction-type and profile ratio tires on all four wheels of your car. This is the safest way to go. If this is not possible, a difference in profile ratios will work, if the construction type is the same.

Tire saving tips

- Break in a new tire gradually. Don't go over 50 miles per hour for the first 50 miles the tire is on the car.
- Check the air pressure regularly when tires are cold; that is, before starting out. Maintain the specified pressure found in the owner's manual.
- When traveling overloaded, or prior to a long trip, inflate your tires properly. This usually means increasing the air pressure. See your owner's manual.
- Drive with anticipation. Avoid jamming on the brakes at traffic lights and intersections. Eliminate jackrabbit starts. Corner at posted speeds. Drive around chuckholes and curbs.
- Check your tires before, during, and after a long trip.
- Do not bleed your tires during a long trip, even if the air pressure increases somewhat.
- Inspect the tires frequently for irregular wear patterns that could signify bad shocks, misalignment, or out-of-balance tires. Keep in mind that most tires are worn out due to defective front end steering parts.
- Check the valve stem and dust cap if the tire is losing air.
- Be sure your spare tire is properly inflated at all times and ready to roll if and when you need it.
- Consolidate your shopping trips around town to make maximum use of your car when it is out. Don't make several trips when one would do.

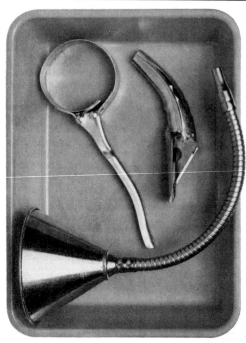

OIL CHANGING GEAR

FLATBLADE AND PHILLIPS-HEAD SCREWDRIVERS

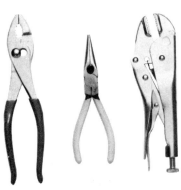

SLIP-JOINT, LONG-NOSE, AND LOCKING-JAW PLIERS

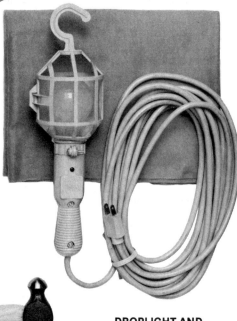

BALL-PEEN HAMMER

DROPLIGHT AND FENDER COVER

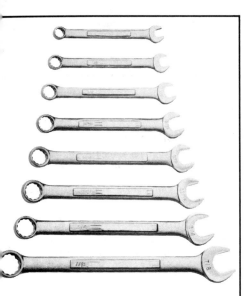

**COMBINATION BOX- AND OPEN-END
WRENCHES**

**RATCHET, SOCKETS, HANDLES, AND
UNIVERSAL JOINT**

ADJUSTABLE WRENCH

Basic Tools

Check your toolbox and compare its contents with the tools shown at the left. If you're missing any, fill in those you don't have before starting to work on your car.

You'll probably want to buy the least expensive tools that will effectively do the job. The very cheapest tool is almost always inadequate. And the very best is superadequate for your purposes. Your best bet is the moderately priced tool. Let's run down the list of basic tools:

Screwdrivers. You'll need at least three flatblade types—small, medium, and large, and a stubby screwdriver helps you work in tight places. You can get by with two Phillips-heads—a #2 and a stubby one.

Pliers. Your toolbox should have at least three: a 6- to 8-inch long slip-joint steel pliers; long-nose pliers about six inches long; and a pair of locking-jaw pliers.

Adjustable wrench. One's enough. Use it when you can't carry a complete set of fixed-opening wrenches with you or for turning nuts and bolts of odd sizes.

Ratchet wrenches and sockets. Actually you'll need only one or two ratchet handles to turn your many sockets. Sockets come in standard depths for most nuts and deep sizes for removing spark plugs and nuts that have a lot of bolt sticking out from them. A universal socket is handy when a bolt or nut is difficult to reach.

Combination wrenches. One end is a box wrench, the other an open-end wrench. With a box wrench, you can apply more torque to a tight nut or bolt without the risk of the wrench slipping off. An open-end wrench, however, slips easily over a nut or bolt. It pays to buy a complete set.

Ball-peen hammer. This is the basic hammer for auto mechanics. Get a good one with a 8-, 12-, or 16-ounce head.

Droplight. You'll need either a standard droplight (shown) or one of the newer fluorescent tubes, which are more expensive but safer.

Fender cover. It's expensive, but useful. If you don't want to spend the money for the professional type, use an old shower curtain, blanket or beach towel.

Oil changing gear. You'll need a drain pan (get one large enough to hold all your car's oil and then some), an oil filter wrench, a flexible-neck tunnel (for transmission fluid), and a combination opener and pour spout.

About Automotive Parts

Buying Tips

Car parts come from a number of sources. Many parts can be purchased at your local service station, or from a new car dealer. But some parts, such as cylinder heads and fenders, you can only get new from a new car dealer, or used from a wrecker. When a car is new, you may want to get factory OEM—Original Equipment Manufacturer—parts to be certain you keep your warranty in force, even if the particular repair is not something that can be done under warranty.

Jobbers

Auto parts jobbers supply most of the parts bought by local service stations and the smaller professional repair shops. They have two prices for everything—a mechanic's price and a retail price. Since perhaps 30 percent of their business is now cash-over-the-counter from do-it-yourself mechanics, they will most likely grant you the mechanic's price once you become known to them.

Parts jobbers are a good source of parts and tools because you are dealing with professionals. They know a lot more about their business—and yours—than a clerk in an auto department or a discount store does, and they will usually help you get good quality parts to do the job.

The prices, with the discount, will be about average. They run a bit higher than those charged by department stores, discount houses, and mail-order auto specialty houses, but they are lower than prices at new car dealers and service stations.

In addition to parts, most of the best jobber shops also run machine shops. They can completely rebuild an engine, turn a brake drum, rebuild a cylinder head, boil out a cylinder block, turn down a crankshaft, fit bearings, assemble press-fitted parts—in short they handle all the jobs the smaller shops farm out. By farming out your work to them directly, you save the commission on the deal which would be collected by the garage or service shop as part of their repair fee. And if there is some specialized machine work you require, the jobber shop knows where to get it done.

Auto specialty stores

Auto speciality stores are another source of parts and tools. Their prices are generally lower. They are better for dress-up or trim items than for hard parts like wheel bearings or ignition points.

Speed shops

Speed shops or custom car shops can be a good source of special parts or specialized machine shop services. On some things their prices will be on a par with, or cheaper than, your local jobbers. They specialize in hot rod work, and if that is your major interest, they are the place to go with your business.

Department and discount stores

Auto departments in department or discount stores offer about the lowest prices for most parts and tools you will find anywhere. The quality of branded, known merchandise is okay and, especially when bought on sale, you can get many things at true bargain prices. The best things to buy here are sealed cans of antifreeze, motor oil by the case (but watch out for brand names that look familiar but are a little different from the known brand), and fast-moving parts that require frequent replacement such as oil filters, air filters, and ignition parts. Brand name spark plugs can also be an excellent deal.

Local auto departments of the big mail-order houses offer the lure of one-stop auto supply shopping and usually have good quality parts at prices very little higher than the super discounters. These are also good places to look for tools on sale. You may be able to get a $15 wrench set for $9.95 when an equivalent quality tool set would cost $20 at the parts jobber.

Mail order

Mail order opens the shelves of some of the largest auto parts suppliers to you at very reasonable prices. Even considering that you must pay postage on top of the catalog prices, you can do very well at a mail-order house. The only drawback in dealing with one is the wait while your order is being filled. Between one and three weeks for delivery to your door is par for the course, with most orders arriving in under two weeks. If you know ahead of time what equipment or parts you need for a specific job, mail order is a good way to go. The catalogs often list parts you will not find on a jobber's shelves or even in a mail-order store's local auto department.

New or rebuilt?

At all of these parts stores, you have a choice of buying new or rebuilt parts. It is usually better to buy some items new, such as brake shoes, heater motors, water pumps, clutch pressure plates, and voltage regulators. A lot depends on the quality of the rebuilding shop. Some remanufacturers, as they like to call themselves, produce parts that are definitely better than new. Check both the price and the guarantee that comes with the parts. The higher the price and the better the guarantee, the higher the quality of the component. Super low prices on rebuilt parts usually indicate poorer workmanship that will show up in shorter life and earlier failures than in higher-priced remanufactured items.

Wrecking yards

Auto wrecking yards can be a superior source for a number of the parts you will be needing—particularly if yours is an older-model car. Most of the better yards are tied in with others across the country by teletype, so there is an excellent chance they can get something for you that would be hard to come by through other sources.

With respect to mechanical parts, wreckers are a good source for engines, transmissions, complete rear axle assemblies, wheels, tires, batteries, starters, and generators or alternators. Most of these parts will come with a guarantee stating that you can exchange them for another if they do not work. Engines will be guaranteed not to have cracked blocks or to burn excessive amounts of oil, for example.

If your car is old it may make little economic sense to put a new or rebuilt engine in it. But an engine from a low-mileage wreck could extend the usefulness of the car for another couple of years at half the cost of a rebuilt engine. In other words, if your car has a life expectancy,

when repaired, of another 25,000 miles, why give it a 50,000-mile engine?

Body parts, especially doors, fenders, hoods, deck lids, seats, trim, light fixtures, and steering wheels, are better than new ones when bought used. Better than new ones? If you buy a new door, you get just that, the door, in prime and without any other parts. You have to remove the latches, hinges, chrome trim, window mechanism, inside trim panel, and weather stripping, from your bent or rusted-out door and install them on the new one. Then you have to paint it to match your car. A used door can be checked for dents and rust, and, with a little bit of luck, you may be able to find one already painted the right color to match your car. The price will be about half to two-thirds of a new door. And putting it in your car will be a lot less work than installing a new one.

Parts that are usually not worth getting from wrecking yards include voltage regulators, windshield wiper motors, carburetors, and similar parts that may have been weather-damaged from outside storage, and which will cost negligibly less than rebuilt parts. As a general rule of thumb, used parts should cost about half as much as new ones.

Replacement glass, particularly windshields, is probably the worst deal at a wrecking yard. The price is hardly less than new glass because of the labor required to remove it. Glass is scarce in the wrecking yard because so much is broken before the cars even arrive. Rear axles are a good deal. The demand for them is low because they rarely break. Yet the supply is good because they often survive in good condition when the rest of the car does not.

Now, you are in business. You know where to get the tools and parts required to do any repair or maintenance job you might care to tackle, and how to do it in a businesslike and safe manner.

Every job you undertake will teach you something about your car and yourself. And as you become more experienced, you will learn how to do your own maintenance as well or better than the pros can do it for you, and at far less cost.

Cleaning parts

Whenever you work on a car, you will always

have greasy, dirty parts to be cleaned. When you first start out, you will need a lot of rags or paper towels. One way to get good disposable wipes for free is to save used paper towels. A basket or paper bag in the kitchen will quickly collect as many as you can use. Even though they've been used for hand drying and are thrown in the bag wrinkled and damp, they dry into just what you need for wiping out an oil drain plug or a valve cover.

Once you progress beyond the point where a few secondhand towels will cover your cleaning needs, you have a couple of parts cleaning choices. You can cut the inside out of a 10-quart square can like the ones bulk oil comes in, fold over the edges so you do not cut yourself, and then use either kerosene or diesel fuel and an old paint brush—or a new parts washing brush at about a buck—for your basic parts cleaning.
CAUTION: Never use gasoline as a parts washing liquid. There are a number of cases in which people have been severely, sometimes fatally, burned when a spark set off the fumes. Even if you work outdoors, there is no way you can safely work with a liquid as volatile and flammable as gasoline.

An even better parts cleaning system is to go the professional route. For not too much money, you can get a five-gallon pail of parts cleaning solution complete with a perforated basket to immerse small parts or hold one end of big ones while you wash them down with the brush. These solutions are emulsifiers that turn grease to soap when you hose down the cleaned parts with water. They are non-flammable and do a fine cleaning job. Rubber gloves are a good idea when you use them because the phenolics used are hard on the hands.

A solution of one of the strong detergents used for cleaning kitchen floors, mixed in an old plastic dishpan, is another good way for a home mechanic to clean parts safely and effectively.

How clean should mechanical parts be before you put them back together? About as clean as freshly washed tableware and dishes. Many early parts failures in major work done by home mechanics are caused by dirt installed with the component when it was assembled by working on a dirty bench in a dusty area. This has even been known to happen in jobs done by professional mechanics.

One thing you can do to make your job easier is to keep your engine really clean. There are spray cans of engine degreasers available from almost all auto parts sources that will do this job effectively. You simply spray them on the engine after covering the distributor cap and carburetor, then hose them off. If you are working in your own driveway, put down a generous layer of old newspapers to catch the dirt. This way, you will not have a black spot on the gravel for the next couple of years.

Another place to clean your engine is at one of the numerous do-it-yourself car washes which have drains capable of handling the residue.

Tire
Rotation Chart

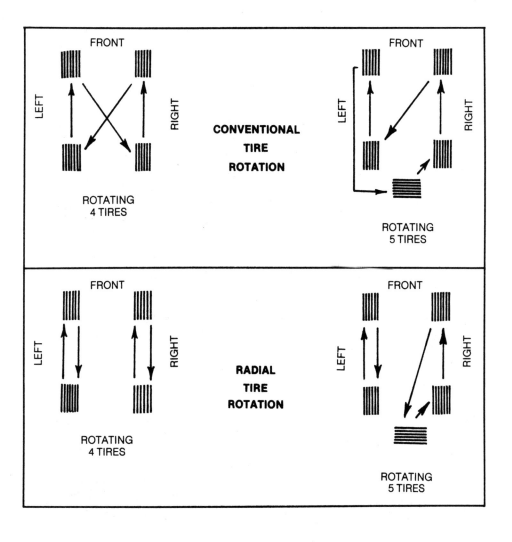

CONVENTIONAL
TIRE
ROTATION

RADIAL
TIRE
ROTATION

Index

T

V

W